RAINER MARIA RILKE 1925

RAINER MARIA RILKE

LETTERS
TO A YOUNG POET

TRANSLATED, WITH AN INTRODUCTION
AND COMMENTARY BY
REGINALD SNELL

DOVER PUBLICATIONS, INC.
Mineola, New York

Bibliographical Note

This Dover edition, first published in 2002, is an unabridged republication of the edition published by Sidgwick and Jackson, London, in 1945.

International Standard Book Number

ISBN-13: 978-0-486-42245-9
ISBN-10: 0-486-42245-3

Manufactured in the United States by Courier Corporation
42245307
www.doverpublications.com

CONTENTS

TRANSLATOR'S PREFACE

I HAVE thought it best to group all the explanations which any letters of Rilke necessarily involve, at the end of the book and out of the way; indeed, no harm will be done if the ordinary reader ignores them altogether, and enjoys the letters simply for what they are. But the student will probably care to pursue further some of the astonishing wealth of ideas which the poet here raises.

The translation is designedly very literal, and the nature of German prose is such that an English rendering which aims—as this does—at close correspondence rather than happy paraphrase, can hardly avoid displaying at times a certain stiffness in the joints; but I have thought it right to reproduce Rilke's oddities of expression and punctuation, which are no less curious in the original than they must seem here; and never to succumb to the temptation to write pretty-sounding English just because it is a poet that speaks. Rilke is a master of the unlikely, but poetically true, word; and a cunning employer of alliteration, personification, and hypallage.

The frontispiece portrait of Rilke is here reproduced by kind permission of Frau M. Weininger, who took the snapshot near Muzot, Switzerland, in 1925. The photographs of the poet hitherto published in England have represented him in moods varying from dogged seriousness to the profoundest dejection, and I take pleasure in producing this evidence that Rilke knew how to smile.

I wish to express my gratitude for the generous and scholarly help afforded me by Dr Julian Hirsch, who has taught me much German.

R. S.

TRANSLATOR'S INTRODUCTION

SINCE Rilke's death in 1926 the publication of his letters has proceeded steadily, in a somewhat haphazard way (the number of letters to a volume varying between two and two hundred), until well over a thousand in all have been given, mainly by his publisher Kippenberg and his son-in-law Carl Sieber, to the world. The central collection contains varied correspondence covering the years 1899-1926 (the time of his first Russian visit to his last days at Muzot); there are the letters to his publisher, covering twenty years' friendly business association; there are the numerous letters quoted, wholly or in part, in various memoirs; and finally, two small collections, the ten early *Letters to a young poet* here translated, and the nine later *Letters to a young woman*. These last two volumes are examples of the care and solicitude which he always shewed to unknown correspondents; Rilke was the postal confessor, for at least a quarter of a century, of a large number of young people. The recipients of the letters in the main series number more than two hundred, and there are many private bundles of letters—beautifully phrased, beautifully penned, intimate talks to people he had never seen—that will in all probability never be published. The poet himself stated, at the end of his life, that he had put into his letters a part of his creative genius; and certainly he is with the great poet letter-writers of European literature, with Goethe and Shelley—almost with Keats. The *Letters to a young poet* illustrate perfectly the kindliness, the complexity, and at the same time the impersonality and remoteness of Rilke's manner with unknown correspondents. He talks repeatedly of his "dear Herr Kappus", but he is really speaking at, not to, the young man; he is thinking aloud, meditating his own problem, spinning—as always, and as he counsels his young poet to do—his web of creation from his own inwards. A young man or woman had only to write him a letter containing the words art, or work, or love, or death, or God (and young people find it very difficult to keep these words out of their letters) in order to touch Rilke into activity. In such letters he always displays modesty, gentleness and a desire to yield, as well as accept, the secrets of the heart; his advice is usually very sound, and a constant feature of his homiletics is his moral sure-footedness. Of the ten letters that follow, nine were written within the space of eighteen months, which were also months of important development for Rilke himself. It is here that much of their interest lies : they contain the *leitmotivs* that were to appear later in his greatest poetry, and nearly all orders in the Rilkean creation are represented, except the angels and the youthfully dead—here, at least, are Solitude, and Difficult Love, and Seeing, and Things, and the Building of God.

It will be well to recapitulate, as briefly as possible, the events in the poet's life that preceded his first letter to a young lieutenant in the Austrian army. René Rilke was born at Prague in 1875, the delicate seven-months' child of a father who fussed and a mother who coddled him ; yet he was destined from birth to be a soldier. From the age of ten he spent four years at a junior, and six months at a senior, Military Academy, where he was bullied and unhappy, and first began to build his defence-works of solitude. He finished his studies at home, where he published his earliest verses, which are musical, cleverly rhymed and glib in the Humbert Wolfe manner. Stefan George, on the single occasion of their meeting in Florence, told him that he had published too early ; "how very very right he was there !" Rilke later wrote (*Letters 1921–1926*, p. 61). All the conceptions which were to prove most fertile for his art seem to have their origin before 1900 : maidenhood, solitude, private death, and God as created not creator. By the turn of the century, and his twenty-fifth birthday, he had published *Laral Offering*, Heinesque and bitter-sweet verses largely concerned with Prague ; *Dream Crowned,* where he begins to brood over death ; *Advent,* which shews new literary influences, including those of Jacobsen and Dehmel ; *To Celebrate Myself,* where the authentic poet in him

4

begins to make himself heard; various early dramas, stories and sketches, some of these last being of a gothically grisly character; and he had written, in a single night, a piece which was to become his Rachmaninoff C♯ minor Prelude—his famous prose-poem *Cornet*.

Before 1903, when young Kappus first wrote to him, Rilke had been subjected to three further influences which were of decisive importance for his life: Russia, Worpswede, and Rodin. Russia was incomparably the most important: it was then that solitude took on a new and deeper meaning for him, and there that he discovered the Neighbour God. He learnt enough of the language to translate Chekhov and Lermontov, and ever after-wards regarded that "remote and sorrowful land", with apparent velleity, as his spiritual home. At Worpswede, an artists' colony near Bremen, he met the "fair-haired painter" Paula Becker, who inspired the most splendid of his *Requiems*, and the sculptor Clara Westhof, a pupil of Rodin's, whom he married in 1901, and with whom he settled down to love (and work) in a cottage. But this idyll did not last long: when their daughter was only six months old, Rilke's allowance from his father suddenly ceased, and he moved to Paris (where Clara later joined him), with a commission to write a monograph on Rodin. He had now published his *Stories of God*, obviously conceived in Russia, subtle-simple tales told with a humour that occasionally borders on archness; his *Book of Images*, containing some of his best lyrics, in which his own poetic voice is unmis-takable all through; and he had written the first two parts of his *Book of Hours*, the *Book of Monkish Life* and the *Book of Pilgrimage*, a catena of meditative poems of great power and beauty about the meaning and the longing of man for God, and of God for man.

He fell heavily under the spell of Rodin; but Paris appalled and terrified him. After the spaciousness and peace of "holy Russia", the solemn talk of Art at Worpswede, and the months of quiet living in his Westerwede cottage, the noise and squalor and cruelty of a great town were torture to him. Writing a little later to Lou Andreas-Salomé, he compared it to the Military Academy—and he could not say worse than that. "Often before going to sleep I read the thirtieth chapter of the Book of Job, and it was all true of me, word for word" (*Letters 1902-1906*, p. 98). He had a lifelong horror of machines; he found railway tunnels "agonizing" and had a "deep dread of enormous towns". He often longed for Russia, which Maurice Baring somewhere sums up as "a plain, a church and a mill". Years afterwards his horror was distilled in the alembic of *Malte Laurids Brigge* into descriptions of disease, abjectness, and violence that have their only parallel in the depths of Dostoevsky. He had been in Paris for some five months when the correspondence with Kappus begins, and the young man may now be left to introduce the letters in his own modest fashion.

INTRODUCTION BY THE YOUNG POET

It was in the late autumn of 1902—I was sitting in the park of the Military Academy in Wiener-Neustadt, beneath some ancient chestnut trees, and was reading a book. I was so engrossed in reading that I hardly noticed how I was joined by the only non-officer among our professors, the learned and kind-hearted parson of the Academy, Horaček. He took the volume out of my hand, looked at the wrapper and shook his head. "Poems by Rainer Maria Rilke?" he asked meditatively. He turned over the leaves here and there, glanced through a few verses, gazed thoughtfully into the distance and finally nodded. " So then the pupil René Rilke has become a poet."

And I learnt about the thin, pale-faced boy whom his parents had sent to the Military Unterrealschule in Sankt-Pölten more than fifteen years previously, so that he might later become an officer. At that time Horaček had been employed there as chaplain, and he still remembered his former pupil distinctly. He depicted him as a quiet, solemn, highly capable boy who liked to keep himself apart, bore the restrictions of a boarder's life patiently, and after his fourth year moved on with the others to the Military Oberrealschule which was situated in Mährisch-Weisskirchen. There, however, his constitution proved insufficiently resilient, and so his parents removed him from the institution and let him continue his studies at home in Prague. Horaček could report no further on the course which his outward life had thereafter taken.

After all this it may be easily understood that I resolved in that very hour to send my poetical efforts to Rainer Maria Rilke and ask for his opinion. Being not yet twenty years old and barely on the threshold of a profession which I felt to be directly opposed to my inclinations, I hoped *to find understanding, if anywhere at all, in the writer of the poems* To Celebrate Myself. *And without my actually having wished it, my verses came to be accompanied by a covering letter in which I revealed myself without reserve as I have never done before or since to another human being.*

Many weeks went by before an answer came. The blue-sealed communication bore the post mark of Paris, weighed heavy in the hand and shewed on the envelope the same clear, beautiful and firm characters [1] *in which the text was set down from the first line to the last. With that began my regular correspondence with Rainer Maria Rilke, which lasted until 1908 and then gradually trickled into nothing, since life drove me off into regions against which the poet's warm, delicate and touching solicitude had really tried to guard me.*

But that is not important. The only thing of importance is the ten letters which here follow, important for the appreciation of the world in which Rainer Maria Rilke lived and worked, and important too for many who are now growing up and developing, today and tomorrow. And where a great and unique man speaks, small men must keep silence.

FRANZ XAVER KAPPUS,

BERLIN, *June* 1929,

THE LETTERS

I

Dear Sir,

your letter reached me only a few days ago. I want to thank you for its great and welcome trust. I can hardly say more. I cannot go into the quality of your verses; for I am too far removed from every kind of critical intention.[2] In making contact with a work of art nothing serves so ill as words of criticism: the invariable result is more or less happy misunderstandings. Things are not all so comprehensible and utterable as people would mostly have us believe; most events are unutterable, consummating themselves in a sphere where word has never trod, and more unutterable than them all are works of art, whose life endures by the side of our own that passes away.

Having written this note by way of introduction, may I just go on to tell you that your verses have no individual quality, but rather, quiet and hidden tendencies to something personal. I feel this most clearly in the last poem *My Soul*. And in the beautiful poem *To Leopardi* there is perhaps growing up a kind of relationship with that great and solitary man. All the same, the poems are not yet anything in themselves, nothing independent, not even the last one or the one to Leopardi. Your friendly letter which accompanied them did not fail to explain to me a number of deficiencies which I felt in reading your verses, without however being able to give a name to them.

You ask if your verses are good. You ask me. You have previously asked others. You send them to journals. You compare them with other poems, and you are troubled when certain editors reject your efforts. Now (as you have permitted me to advise you) I beg you to give all that up. You are looking outwards, and of all things that is what you must now not do. Nobody can advise and help you, nobody. There is only one single means. Go inside yourself. Discover the motive that bids you write; examine whether it sends its roots down to the deepest places of your heart, confess to yourself whether you would have to die if writing were denied you. This before all: ask yourself in the quietest hour of your night: *must* I write? Dig down into yourself for a deep answer. And if this should be in the affirmative, if you may meet this solemn question with a strong and simple "*I must*", then build your life according to this necessity; your life must, right to its most unimportant and insignificant hour, become a token and a witness of this impulse. Then draw near to Nature. Then try, as if you were one of the first men, to say what you see and experience and love and lose. Do not write love poems; avoid at first those forms which are too familiar and usual: they are the most difficult, for great and fully matured strength is needed to make an individual contribution where good and in part brilliant traditions exist in plenty. Turn therefore from the common themes to those which your own everyday life affords; depict your sorrows and desires, your passing thoughts and belief in some kind of beauty —depict all that with heartfelt, quiet, humble sincerity and use to express yourself the things that surround you, the images of your dreams and the objects of your memory. If your everyday life seems poor to you, do not accuse it; accuse yourself, tell yourself you are not poet enough to summon up its riches; since for the creator there is no poverty and no poor or unimportant place. And even if you were in a prison whose walls allowed none of the sounds of the world to reach your senses— would you not still have always your childhood,[3] that precious, royal richness, that treasure house of memories? Turn your attention there. Try to raise the submerged sensations of that distant past; your personality will grow stronger, your solitude will extend itself and will become a twilit dwelling which the noise of others passes by in the distance.—And if from this turning inwards, from this sinking into your private world, there come verses, you will not think to ask anyone whether they are good verses. You will not attempt, either, to interest journals in these works: for you will see in them your own dear genuine posses-sion, a portion and a voice of your life. A work of art is good if it has grown out of necessity. In this manner of its origin lies its true estimate: there is no other. Therefore, my dear Sir, I could give you no advice but this: to go into yourself and to explore the depths whence your life wells forth; at its source you will find the answer to the question whether you *must* create. Accept it as it sounds, without enquiring too closely into every word. Perhaps it will turn out that you are called to be an artist. Then take your fate upon yourself and bear it, its burden and its greatness, without ever asking for that reward which might come from without. For the creator must be a world for himself, and find everything within himself, and in Nature to which he has attached himself.

Perhaps however, after this descent into yourself and into your aloneness, you will have to renounce your claim to become a poet; (it is sufficient, as I have said, to feel that one could live without writing, in order not to venture it at all.) But even then this introversion which I beg of you has not been in vain. Your life will at all events find thenceforward its individual paths; and that they may be good and rich and far reaching I wish for you more than I can say.

What more shall I say to you? Everything seems to me to have its proper emphasis; I would finally just like to advise you to grow through your development quietly and seriously; you can interrupt it in no more violent manner than by looking outwards, and expecting answer from outside to questions which perhaps only your innermost feeling in your most silent hour can answer.

It was a joy to me to find the name of Professor Horaček in your letter; I retain a great admiration for that dear and learned man, and a gratitude that persists through the years. Will you please tell him of this sentiment of mine; it is very good of him still to remember me, and I know how to appreciate it.

The verses which you kindly entrusted to me I am returning at the same time as this. And I thank you again for the magnitude and cordiality of your trust; in this answer, given with sincerity and to the best of my knowledge, I have sought to make myself a little worthier of it than, as a stranger, I actually am.

With every respect and sympathy:

RAINER MARIA RILKE.

II

VIAREGGIO [4] near PISA (ITALY), *April 5th* 1903.

You must forgive me, my dear and honoured Sir, for not gratefully remembering your letter of February 24th before today: I was suffering the whole time, not exactly from an illness, but oppressed by an influenza-like exhaustion which made me incapable of anything. And finally, when it would not improve, I came to this southerly sea, whose benefit has helped me before now. But I am not yet well, I find writing difficult, and so you must take these few lines in lieu of more.

You must of course know that you will always give me pleasure with every letter, and be only indulgent towards the answer, which will often perhaps leave you empty handed; for fundamentally, and precisely in the deepest and most important things, we are unspeakably alone, and a great deal must happen in order that one man may be able to advise or even help another—a great deal must succeed, a whole constellation of things must be realized for it once to prosper.

I wanted to say two further things to you today: irony:

Do not let yourself be governed by it, especially not in un-productive moments. In productive ones try to make use of it as one more means of seizing life. Used purely, it is itself pure, and one need not be ashamed of it; and when you feel too familiar with it, when you fear the growing intimacy with it, then turn towards great and serious subjects, before which it becomes small and helpless. Seek for the depth of things: there irony never descends—and when you have thus brought it to the edge of greatness, test at the same time whether this mode of perception springs from a necessity of your being. For under the influence of serious things it will either fall away from you (if it is something non-essential), or else it will (if it belongs to you innately) with gathering strength become a serious tool and be ranked among the means by which you will have to form your art.

And the second thing that I wanted to tell you today is this: Only a few of all my books are indispensable to me, and two of these are actually always among my things wherever I am. Even here they are round me: the Bible, and the books of the great Danish writer Jens Peter Jacobsen.[5] It occurs to me to wonder whether you know his works. You can easily procure them, for a part of them has appeared in Reclam's Universal Library in a very good translation. Get hold of the little volume called *Six Tales* by J. P. Jacobsen, and his novel *Niels Lyhne*, and start with the first story in the former book, which is called *Mogens*. A world will come over you, the happiness, the wealth, the inconceivable greatness of a world. Live for a while in these books, learn from them what seems to you worth learning, but above all love them. Your love will be repaid a thousand thou-sandfold, and whatever your life may become,—will, I am con-vinced, run through the texture of your growing as one of the most important threads among all the threads of your experi-ences, disappointments and joys.

If I am to say from whom I have learnt anything about the nature of creation, about its depth and everlastingness, there are only two names that I can mention : Jacobsen, that great, great writer, and Auguste Rodin,[6] who has not his peer among all the artists who are alive today.

And may all success attend your ways !

Yours :

RAINER MARIA RILKE.

III

VIAREGGIO [7] near PISA (ITALY), *April 23rd* 1903.

You have given me much pleasure, my dear and honoured Sir, with your Easter letter ; for it said much that was good of yourself, and the way in which you spoke of Jacobsen's great and beloved art shewed me that I was not mistaken when I led your life and its many questions to that abundant source.

Now *Niels Lyhne* will reveal itself to you, a book of splendours and of depths ; the oftener one reads it : everything seems to be in it, from the gentlest possible scents of life to the full, large taste of its heaviest fruits. Nothing is there that had not been understood, conceived, experienced and recognized in the vibrating echo of memory ; no experience has been too slight, and the smallest happening unfolds like a destiny, and the destiny itself is like a wonderful broad tapestry where every thread is inwoven by an infinitely delicate hand, laid next to its fellow, and held and supported by a hundred others. You will experience the great happiness of reading this book for the first time, and will go through its innumerable surprises as in a new dream. But I can tell you that later too one goes again and again through these books, marvelling in the same way, and that they lose nothing of the wonderful power, and surrender nothing of the fairy-tale quality with which they overwhelm the reader at the start.

One only enjoys them ever increasingly, becomes more grateful and somehow better and simpler in one's gazing, deeper in one's believing of life, and in life greater and more blessed.—

And later you must read the wonderful book of the destiny and longing of *Marie Grubbe* and Jacobsen's letters and diaries and fragments, and finally his verses, which (even though they are only moderately well translated) live in everlasting sound. (To that end I would advise you to buy, when you get the chance, the lovely complete edition of Jacobsen's works, which contains all the above. It appeared in three volumes, well translated, published by Eugen Dietrichs of Leipzig, and costs, I rather think, only five or six marks a volume.)

Your opinion of *There should have been roses there* [8] . . . (that work of such incomparable delicacy and form) is of course, in contrast with that expressed in the introduction, quite, quite unimpeachably correct. And let me here at once request you : read as few aesthetic-critical things as possible,—they are either partisan opinions, become hardened and meaningless in their lifeless petrifaction, or else they are a skilful play upon words, in which one view is uppermost today and its opposite tomorrow. Works of art are of an infinite solitariness, and nothing is less likely to bring us near to them than criticism. Only love can apprehend and hold them, and can be just towards them.— Decide each time according to *yourself* and your feelings in the face of every such declaration, discussion or introduction ; if you should still be wrong, the natural growth of your inner life will lead you slowly in the course of time to other perceptions. Let your judgments have their own quiet, undisturbed development, which must, like all progress, come from deep within, and cannot in any way be pressed or hurried. It means everything to carry for the full time and then to bring forth. To allow every impression and every germ of a feeling to grow to completion wholly in yourself, in the darkness, in the unutterable, unconscious, inaccessible to your own understanding, and to await with deep humility and patience the hour of birth of a new clarity: that is alone what living as an artist means: in understanding as in creation.

There is no measuring by time there, a year there has no meaning, and ten years are nothing. To be an artist means: not to reckon and count; to ripen like the tree which does not force its sap and stands confident in the storms of Spring without fear lest no Summer might come after. It does come. But it comes only to the patient ones, who are there as if eternity lay in front of them, so unconcernedly still and far. I am learning it daily, learning it through pains to which I am grateful: patience is all!

RICHARD DEHMEL [9]: I feel about his books (and incidentally about the man too, whom I know slightly) that when I have found one of his lovely pages I am always afraid of the one that follows, which may ruin everything again and turn what is charming into something unworthy. You have characterized him quite well in the phrase "living and writing in heat".—And in point of fact artistic experience really lies so incredibly close to sexual, to its agony and its ecstasy, that both phenomena are actually only different forms of one and the same longing and felicity. And if instead of heat one might speak of—sex, sex in the large, wide, pure sense, without any slur of ecclesiastical error, his art would be very great and infinitely important. His poetic strength is great, and strong as a primitive impulse, it has its own uncompromising rhythms within itself, and gushes out as if from a mountain side.

But it seems that this strength is not always quite sincere and without pose. (But that is just one of the most difficult tests with a creator: he must always remain unconscious, unsuspecting of his best virtues, if he does not want to deprive them of their unselfconsciousness and integrity!) And then, when it comes rushing through his being into sexuality, it finds there a man not quite so pure as it required him to be. There it sees no entirely mature and unmixed sex world, but one which is not human enough, merely masculine, which is heat, intoxication and restlessness, and loaded with the old prejudices and arrogances with which men have disfigured and burdened love. Because he loves only as man, not as human being, there is in his sexual feelings something narrow, seemingly wild, malicious, temporal, finite, which weakens his art and makes it equivocal and dubious. It is not without blemish, it bears the imprint of time and of passion, and little of it will endure and persist. (But most art is like that!) But nevertheless we can deeply enjoy what is great in it, only we must not get lost over it and become adherents of that Dehmel world which is so infinitely frightening, full of adultery and confusion, far from the real destinies which make us suffer more than these temporal glooms, but also give us more opportunity for greatness and more courage for eternity.

Finally, as far as my books are concerned, I should like best to send you all that could give you any pleasure. But I am very poor, and my books, as soon as they have once appeared, belong no more to me. I cannot buy them myself—and, as I should so often like, give them to those who would be good to them.

Therefore I am writing out for you on a slip of paper the titles (and publishers) of my most recent books (the latest, I have published some twelve or thirteen in all), and must leave it to you, dear Sir, to procure some of them for yourself at your leisure.

I am glad to know that my books are in your hands.
Goodbye

Yours:

RAINER MARIA RILKE.

IV

Temporarily at WORPSWEDE [10] near BREMEN,
July 16th 1903.

I left Paris about ten days ago, badly ailing and tired, and came to a great northern plain, whose remoteness and silence and sky are to make me well again. But I ran into a long spell of rain, which has only today begun to clear a little over the restlessly waving land; and I am using this first moment of brightness to send you, dear Sir, my greetings.

My dear Herr Kappus: I have left a letter of yours long unanswered, not that I had forgotten it—on the contrary: it was of the kind that one reads again when one finds it among other letters, and I recognized you in it as if you were close at hand. It was the letter of May 2nd, and you doubtless remember it. When I read it, as I do now, in the great stillness of this faraway place, your beautiful concern for life moves me even more than I experienced it in Paris, where everything has a different ring and dies away by reason of the monstrous noise that makes all things tremble. Here, where a vast countryside is around me, over which the winds come in from the seas, here I feel that there is nowhere a human being who can answer you those questions and feelings which have a life of their own within their depths; for even the best men go astray with words, when these are to express something very gentle and almost unutterable. But I believe nevertheless that you need not be left without some solution, if you hold to things similar to those on which my eyes now take their recreation. If you hold to Nature, to the simplicity that is in her, to the small detail that scarcely one man sees, which can so unexpectedly grow into something great and boundless; if you have this love for insignificant things and seek, simply as one who serves, to win the confidence of what seems to be poor: then everything will become easier for you, more coherent and somehow more conciliatory, not perhaps in the understanding, which lags wondering behind, but in your innermost consciousness, wakefulness and knowing. You are so young, you have not even begun, and I would like to beg you, dear Sir, as well as I can, to have patience with everything that is unsolved in your heart and to try to cherish the questions themselves, like closed rooms and like books written in a very strange tongue. Do not search now for the answers which cannot be given you because you could not live them. It is a matter of living everything. Live the questions now. Perhaps you will then gradually, without noticing it, one distant day live right into the answer. Perhaps indeed you carry within yourself the possibility of shaping and forming, as a particularly pure and blessed kind of life; train yourself for it—but take what comes in complete trust, if only it comes from your will, from some inner need of yours, take it to yourself and do not hate anything. Sex is difficult; yes. But it is the difficult that is enjoined upon us, almost everything serious is difficult,[11] and everything is serious. If you only recognize that and contrive, yourself, out of your own disposition and nature, out of your experience and childhood and strength to achieve an entirely individual relationship to sex (not influenced by convention and custom), then you need no longer fear to lose yourself and become unworthy of your best possession.

Bodily delight is a sense experience, just like pure seeing or the pure feeling with which a lovely fruit fills the tongue; it is a great boundless experience which is given us, a knowing of the world, the fullness and the splendour of all knowing. Our acceptance of it is not bad; what is bad is that almost all men misuse and squander this experience, and apply it as a stimulus to the weary places of their life, a dissipation instead of a rallying for the heights. Mankind have turned eating, too, into something else: want on the one hand, and superfluity on the other, have dulled the clarity of this need, and all those deep, simple necessities by which life renews itself have become similarly dull. But the individual can clarify them for himself and live clearly, (or if not the individual, who is too dependent, then at any rate the solitary man.) He can remember that all beauty in animals and plants is a quiet enduring form of love and longing, and he can see the animal, as he sees the plant, patiently and willingly uniting and propagating itself and growing, not from physical lust, not from physical pain, but bowing to necessities which are greater than lust and pain and more powerful than will and opposition. O that man might be more humble in accepting this secret of which the earth is full even in its tiniest creatures, and more sincere in bearing, enduring and feeling how frightfully serious it is, instead of taking it lightly. That he might be reverent towards his fertility, which is all one whether it be intellectual or physical; for intellectual creation too derives from the physical, is of one substance with it, it is only like a gentler, more enraptured and everlasting repetition of bodily delight. "The thought of being a creator, of begetting and forming" is nothing without its continual great confirmation and realization in the world, nothing without the thousandfold assent from things and animals,—and its enjoyment is so indescribably beautiful and rich only because it is full of inherited memories of the begetting and bearing of millions. In one creator's thought a thousand forgotten nights of love revive again and fill it full of loftiness and grandeur. Those who come together in the night time and entwine in swaying delight perform a serious work and gather up sweetness, depth and strength for the song of some poet that is to be, who will rise to tell of unspeakable bliss. And they summon the future; and even though they go astray and embrace blindly, yet the future comes, a new human being arises, and on the basis of the chance occurrence which here seems consummated, awakens the law by which a resistant vigorous seed forces its way to the egg-cell that advances openly to meet it. Do not let yourself be misled by outward appearances; in the depths everything becomes law. And those who live the secret falsely and badly (and they are very many) only lose it for themselves and yet hand it on like a sealed letter, without knowing it. And do not be confused by the multiplicity of names and the complexity of instances. Perhaps there is over everything a great motherhood, as a common longing. The loveliness of the virgin, a being that (as you so beautifully say) "has not yet accomplished anything", is motherhood fore-boding and preparing itself, uneasy and yearning. And the mother's beauty is serving motherhood, and in the old woman there is a great memory. And in the man too there is mother-hood, it seems to me, physical and spiritual; his begetting is also a kind of birth-giving, and it is birth-giving when he creates out of his innermost fullness. And perhaps the sexes are more akin than we suppose, and the great renewal of the world will perhaps consist in this, that man and maiden, freed from all false feelings and perversions, will seek each other not as opposites but as brother and sister, as neighbours, and will unite as human beings to bear in common, simply, seriously and patiently, the heavy sex that has been laid upon them.

But everything that once perhaps will be possible to many, the solitary man can already prepare for and build now with his hands, which go less astray. Therefore, dear Sir, love your solitude [12] and bear the pain which it has caused you with fair-sounding lament. For those that are near you are far, you say, and this shews that distance begins to grow round you. And when your nearness is far, then your distance is already among the stars and very great; be glad of your growing, into which you can take no one else with you, and be good to those that remain behind, and be self-possessed and quiet with them and do not torment them with your doubts and do not frighten them with your confidence or joy, which they could not com-prehend. Seek some unpretending and honest communion with them, which you are under no necessity to alter when you yourself become more and more different; love life in a strange guise in them, and make allowance for those ageing people who fear the solitude in which you trust. Avoid furnishing material for the drama which is always impending between parents and children; it uses up much of the children's strength and wastes away the love of their elders, which is operative and warm even when it does not comprehend. Demand no advice from them and reckon with no understanding; but believe in a love that is preserved for you like a heritage, and trust that in this love there is a strength and a blessing which you are not bound to leave behind you though you may travel far!

It is good that you are entering first of all upon a profession which makes you independent and places you on your own in every sense. Wait patiently to see whether your innermost life feels constrained by the form of this profession. I consider it a very difficult one and a hard taskmaster, as it is burdened with much convention and gives hardly any scope to a personal inter-pretation of its tasks. But your solitude will be your home and haven even in the midst of very strange conditions, and from there you will discover all your paths. All my wishes are ready to accompany you, and my trust is with you.

Yours:

RAINER MARIA RILKE.

V

ROME,[13] *October 29th* 1903.

DEAR AND HONOURED SIR,

I received your letter of August 29th in Florence, and now—a whole two months later—I am telling you of it. Do forgive this dilatoriness,—but I do not like writing letters while I am on the move, because I need more for letter writing than the absolutely necessary implements: some quiet and solitude and an hour that is not too strange.

We arrived in Rome about six weeks ago, at a time when it

was still the empty, the hot, the fever-discredited Rome, and this circumstance, together with other practical difficulties of settling in, helped to perpetuate the unrest about us, so that the foreignness lay upon us with the weight of homelessness. Add to this that Rome (when you do not yet know it) has a stifling, saddening effect upon you during the first few days: through the inanimate and dismal museum feeling which it exhales, through the multiplicity of its pasts, dragged into view and laboriously maintained pasts (on which a small present supports itself), through the unspeakable over-estimation of all these defaced and dilapidated things, fostered by savants and philologists and imitated by the ordinary tourist to Italy, which are yet fundamentally no more than fortuitous remains of another time and a life that is not ours and should not be ours. Finally after weeks of daily resistance you find your bearings again, although still a little bewildered, and you reflect: no, there is not more beauty here than elsewhere, and all these objects which have been continuously admired for generations, which workmen's hands have mended and restored, signify nothing, are nothing and have no heart and no worth;—but there is much beauty here, because there is much beauty everywhere. Eternally living waters move along the old aqueducts into the great town and dance in the numerous squares over white stone bowls and display themselves in broad capacious basins and murmur by day and increase their murmuring in the night, which here is great and starry and soft with winds. And gardens are here, unforgettable avenues and flights of stairs, stairs devised by Michelangelo, stairs which are built after the pattern of downward gliding waters,—broad in their descent, bringing forth step from step as if they were waves. Through impressions like these you come to yourself, win your way back from the pretentious manifold which talks and chatters there (and how talkative it is!), and you learn slowly to recognize the very few things in which something eternal endures that you can love, and something solitary in which you can gently share.

I am still living in the town, on the capitol, not far from the loveliest equestrian statue that has been preserved to us from Roman art,—that of Marcus Aurelius; but in a few weeks I shall be moving to a quiet unpretentious room, an old pavilion[14] that lies lost quite deep within a large park, hidden from the town, its bustle and hazard. There I shall live the whole winter and rejoice in the great stillness, from which I expect the gift of good and effective hours. . . .

From there, where I shall be more at home, I will write you a longer letter, in which I will also deal with what you wrote to me. Today I must only tell you (and perhaps it is wrong of me not to have done this before) that the book announced in your letter (which was to contain works of your own) has not turned up here. Has it been returned to you, perhaps from Worpswede? (Because parcels may not be forwarded abroad.) That is the happiest possibility, and I should be glad to have it confirmed. I hope there is no question of its loss,—but indeed in the conditions of the Italian postal system that would be no exceptional occurrence—unfortunately.

I should have been glad to receive this book (as I should any token from you); any verses which have come into existence meanwhile (if you will entrust them to me) I will always read and re-read and experience as well and as cordially as I can. With good wishes and greetings

Yours:

RAINER MARIA RILKE.

VI

ROME, December 23rd 1903.

MY DEAR HERR KAPPUS,

you shall not go without a greeting from me now that Christmas is approaching and you are bearing your solitude, in the midst of the festival, more heavily than usual. But when you notice that it is great, be glad of that; for what (you must ask yourself) would solitude be that had not greatness; there is only one solitude, and it is great and is not easy to bear, and to almost everyone there come hours when they would gladly exchange it for some kind of communion, however banal and cheap, for the appearance of some slight harmony with the most easily available, with the most undeserving. . . . But perhaps those are just the hours when solitude grows; for its growing is painful like the growing of boys and sad like the beginning of Spring. But that must not mislead you. What is needed is, in the end, simply this: solitude, great inner solitude. Going into yourself and meeting no one for hours on end,—that is what you must be able to attain. To be alone, as you were alone in childhood,[15] when the grown-ups were going about, involved with things which seemed important and great, because the great ones looked so busy and because you grasped nothing of their business.

And when one day you perceive that their pursuits are paltry, their professions torpid and no longer connected with life, why not proceed like a child to look upon them as something alien, from out of the depth of your own world, out of the spaciousness of your own solitude, which is itself work and status and profession? Why want to exchange a child's wise non-understanding for defensiveness and disdain, when surely non-understanding is aloneness, but defensiveness and disdain are participation in what you want by these means to avoid.

Think, dear Sir, of the world which you carry within yourself, and call this thinking what you like; let it be memory of your own childhood or longing for your own future,—only pay attention to what arises within you, and set it above everything that you notice about you. Your inmost happening is worth your whole love, that is what you must somehow work at, and not lose too much time and too much courage in explaining your attitude to people. Who tells you, anyhow, that you have such a thing at all?—I know your profession is hard and filled with contradiction of yourself, and I anticipated your lament and knew that it would come. Now it has come I cannot appease it, I can only advise you to consider whether all professions are not like that, full of demands, full of hostility against the individual, saturated so to say with the hatred of those who have reconciled themselves mutely and morosely to their own insipid duty. The situation in which you now have to live is no more heavily burdened with convention, prejudice and error than all the other situations, and if there are some which make parade of a greater freedom, there is certainly none which is in itself wide and spacious and related to the great things of which real life consists. Only the individual who is solitary is brought like a thing [16] under the deep laws, and when a man steps out into the morning that is just beginning, or looks out into the evening that is full of happenings, and when he feels what is coming to pass there, then all rank drops from him as from a dead man, although he is standing in the midst of sheer life. What you now, dear Herr Kappus, have to experience as an officer, you would have felt similarly in every profession that exists, even if you had sought only easy and independent contacts in society, apart from any occupation, this oppressive feeling would not have been spared you. It is the same everywhere; but that is no reason for anxiety or depression; if there is no communion between other people and yourself, try to be near things, which will not desert you; the nights are still there, and the winds that go through the trees and over many lands; among things and with the animals everything is still full of happening, in which you may take a part; and the children are still as you were in childhood, as sad and happy—and when you think of your childhood you are living among them again, among the solitary children, and the grown-ups are nothing, and their dignity has no worth.

And if it dismays and torments you to think of childhood and of the simplicity and stillness that goes with it, because you can no longer believe in God who is to be met with everywhere there, ask yourself, dear Herr Kappus, whether you have after all really lost God? [17] Is it not much rather the case that you have never yet possessed him? For when might that have been? Do you believe a child can hold him, him whom men bear only with difficulty, whose weight bows down the aged? Do you believe that one who really has him could lose him like a little stone, or do you not also feel that one who had him could but be lost by him?—But when you realize that he was not in your childhood, and not beforehand, when you surmise that Christ was deluded by his longing and Mohammed betrayed by his pride,—and when you feel with horror that he does not exist now either, in this hour when we are speaking of him,—what entitles you then to miss, as if he had passed away, and to seek, as if he were lost, someone who has never been?

Why do you not think that he who draws near from all eternity is still to come, that he is in the future, the final fruit of a tree whose leaves we are? What prevents you from throwing forward his truth into times yet to be, and living your life as a painful and beautiful day in the history of a great gestation? Do you not see, then, how everything that happens is for ever a beginning, and might it not be His beginning, since beginning is in itself always so beautiful? If he is the most perfect, must not the inferior precede him, that he may choose himself out of abundance and profusion?—Must he not be the last, in order to embrace everything within himself, and what sense should we have if he for whom we crave had already been?

As bees collect honey, so we take what is sweetest out of everything and build Him. We start actually with the slight, with the unpretentious (if only it is done with love), with work and with resting after it, with a silence or with a little solitary joy, with everything that we do alone, without helpers or adherents, we begin him whom we shall not experience any more than our forefathers could experience us. And yet they are in us, those who have long since passed away, as natural disposition, as burden on our destiny, as blood that throbs, and as gesture that rises up out of the depths of time.

Is there anything which can take from you the hope of thus being hereafter in him, in the most distant, the uttermost?

Celebrate Christmas, dear Herr Kappus, in this pious feeling, that He perhaps needs just this fear of life from you in order to begin; these very days of your transition are perhaps the time when everything in you is working upon him, as once before in childhood you worked upon him breathlessly. Be patient and without resentment, and reflect that the least we can do is, not to make his becoming more difficult for him than the earth makes it for the Spring that wants to come.

And be glad and comforted.

Yours:

RAINER MARIA RILKE.

VII

ROME, *May 14th* 1904.

MY DEAR HERR KAPPUS,

much time has passed since I received your last letter. Do not take it ill of me; it was first of all work, then interruption, and finally weakness of health that continuously held me back from this answer, which (so I intended) was to come to you from good and quiet days. Now I feel somewhat better again (the beginning of Spring with its wicked wayward changes touched us badly even here) and find the time, dear Herr Kappus, to greet you and (as I am glad with all my heart to do) to answer this and that point in your letter to the best of my knowledge.

You see: I have copied out your sonnet,[18] because I found it beautiful and simple, and born in the form which it wears with such quiet grace. Those are the best of the verses which you have permitted me to read. And now I am giving you that copy, because I know that it is important and full of new experience to find one's own work again in a strange hand-writing. Read the verses as though they were strange, and you will feel in your innermost self how very much they are yours.— It has been a joy for me to read this sonnet and your letter many times; I thank you for them both.

And you must not let yourself be misled, in your solitude, by the fact that there is something in you which wants to escape from it. This very wish will, if you use it quietly and pre-eminently and like a tool, help to spread your solitude over wide country. People have (with the help of convention) found the solution of everything in ease and the easiest side of ease; but it is clear that we' must hold to the difficult; everything living holds to it, everything in Nature grows and defends itself according to its own character and is an individual in its own right, strives to be so at any cost and against all opposition. We know little, but that we must hold to the difficult is a certainty that will not leave us; it is good to be solitary, for solitude is difficult; the fact that a thing is difficult must be one more reason for our doing it.

To love is also good: for love is difficult.[19] Fondness between human beings: that is perhaps the most difficult task that is set us, the ultimate thing, the final trial and test, the work for which all other work is only preparation. Therefore young people, who are beginners in everything, *cannot* know love yet: they have to learn it. With their whole being, with all their strength gathered about their lonely, fearful, upward beating heart, they must learn to love. But apprenticeship is always a long, secluded time, and therefore loving is for a long while, far into life—: solitude, heightened and deepened aloneness for him who loves. Loving in the first instance is nothing that can be called losing, surrendering and uniting oneself to another (for what would a union be, of something unclarified and unready, still inferior—?), it is a sublime occasion for the individual to mature, to grow into something in himself, to become world for himself for another's sake, it is a great exacting claim upon him, something that chooses him out and summons him to a distant goal. Only in this sense, as a task to work upon themselves ("to hearken and to hammer day and night") might young people use the love that is given them. The self-losing and the surrender and all manner of communion is not for them (they must save and treasure for a long, long while yet), it is the ultimate thing, it is perhaps something for which human lives are so far hardly adequate.

But that is where young people so often and so grievously go wrong: that they (whose nature it is to have no patience) throw themselves at each other when love comes over them, scatter themselves abroad, just as they are in all their untidiness, disorder and confusion . . .: But what is to be done then? How is life to act upon this heap of half crushed matter which they call their communion and which they would dearly like to style their happiness, if that were possible, and their future? So each one loses himself for the other's sake, and loses the other and many others who wanted still to come. And loses the expanses and possibilities, exchanges the drawing near and fleeting away of gentle, presageful things for a sterile helplessness out of which nothing more can come; nothing but a little disgust, disillusion and poverty and deliverance into one of the many conventions which are set up in large numbers as public refuges along this most dangerous of roads. No region of human experience is so well supplied with conventions as this; life-belts of the most varied invention, boats and swimming-bladders are there; social perception has contrived to create shelters of every description, for as it was disposed to take love-life as a pleasure, it had to mould it into something easy, cheap, innocuous and safe, as public pleasures are.

Many young people, to be sure, who love falsely, that is simply surrendering, letting solitude go (the average person will always persist in that way), feel the oppression of failure and want to make the situation in which they find themselves full of vitality and fruitful in their own personal fashion—; for their nature tells them that even less than anything else of importance can the questions of love be resolved publicly and by this or that compromise; that they are questions, intimate questions from one human being to another, which need in every instance a new, particular, purely personal answer—: but how should those who have already confounded themselves and are no longer bounded or separate, who therefore no longer possess anything individual, be able to find a way out of themselves, out of the depth of their already shattered solitude?

They act out of mutual helplessness, and if then they want, with the best of intentions, to avoid the convention that catches their eye (say that of marriage), they end up in the clutches of a less clamorous but equally deadly conventional solution; for there everything all round them is—convention; where it is a question of a hastily fused, turbid communion, every possible action must be conventional; every relationship to which such entanglement leads has its convention, be it as unusual as it may (that is, in the ordinary sense immoral); why, even separation would in such a case be a conventional step, an impersonal random decision without strength and without effect.

Anyone who considers it seriously will find that for difficult love, as for death, which is difficult, no explanation, no solution, neither sign nor path has yet been made known; and for both these tasks which we carry secretly and hand on without uncovering them, no universal rule based on agreed principles can be discovered. But in proportion as we begin to make individual trial of life, these great things will meet us as individuals at closer quarters. The claims which the difficult work of love lays upon our development are more than life-sized, and as beginners we are not equal to them. But if we continue to hold out and take this love upon ourselves as a burden and apprenticeship, instead of losing ourselves in all the light and frivolous play behind which mankind have concealed themselves from the most serious gravity of their existence,—then perhaps some small progress and some alleviation will become perceptible to those who come long after us; that would be much.

We are really only just beginning to regard the relationship of a human individual to another individual dispassionately and objectively, and our attempts to live such a relationship have no pattern before them. And yet in the passage of time there are now several things that are ready to help our shy novitiate.

The girl and the woman in their new, individual unfolding will be only transient imitators of bad or good masculine behaviour, and repeaters of masculine professions. After the uncertainty of such transitions it will be seen that women have passed through the exuberance and vicissitudes of those (often ridiculous) disguises, only in order to purify their most essential being from the distorting influences of the other sex. Surely women, in whom life tarries and dwells more immediately, fruitfully and confidently, must have become fundamentally more mature human beings, more *human* human beings, than light man, whom the weight of no body's fruit pulls down beneath the surface of life, who, conceited and rash as he is, underrates what he thinks he loves. This humanity of woman, brought forth in pains and degradations, will come to light when she has shed the conventions of mere femininity in the alterations of her outward station, and the men who today do not feel it coming will be surprised and struck by it. One day (for this there are already reliable signs speaking and shining, especially in the northern countries [20]), one day the girl will be here and the woman whose name will no longer signify merely the opposite of masculinity, but something in itself, something which makes us think of no complement or limitation, but only of life and existence,—: the feminine human being.

This step forward will (very much against the wishes of out-stripped man to begin with) change the love experience that now is full of error, alter it fundamentally, refashion it into a relationship meant to be between one human being and another, no longer between man and wife. And this more human love (which will consummate itself infinitely thoughtfully and gently, and well and clearly in binding and loosing) will be something like that which we are preparing with struggle and toil, the love which consists in the mutual guarding, bordering and saluting of two solitudes.

And one thing more: do not think that the great love which was once enjoined upon you as a boy, became lost; can you say whether great and good wishes were not then ripening within you, and resolutions by which you live to this day? I believe that this love remains so strong and powerful in your memory because it was your first deep aloneness and the first inner work which you did upon your life.—All good wishes for you, dear Herr Kappus!

Yours:

RAINER MARIA RILKE.

VIII

BORGEBY GÅRD,[21] FLÄDIE, SWEDEN, *August 12th* 1904.

I want to talk to you again for a while, dear Herr Kappus, although I can say almost nothing that is helpful, hardly anything profitable. You have had many great sorrows, which have passed away. And you say that even this passing was difficult and jarring for you. But please consider whether these great sorrows have not rather passed through the midst of yourself? Whether much in you has not altered, whether you have not somehow changed in some part of your being, while you were sorrowful? Only those sorrows are dangerous and bad which we carry about among our fellows in order to drown them; like diseases which are superficially and foolishly treated, they only recede and break out after a short interval all the more frightfully; and gather themselves in our inwards, and are life, are unlived, disdained, lost life, of which one can die. If it were possible for us to see further than our knowledge extends and out a little over the outworks of our surmising, perhaps we should then bear our sorrows with greater confidence than our joys. For they are the moments when something new, something unknown, has entered into us; our feelings grow dumb with shy confusion, everything in us retires, a stillness supervenes, and the new thing that no one knows stands silent there in the midst.

I believe that almost all our sorrows are moments of tension which we experience as paralysis, because we no longer hear our estranged feelings living. Because we are alone with the strange thing that has entered into us; because for a moment everything familiar and customary has been taken from us; because we stand in the middle of a crossing where we cannot remain standing. Therefore it is, also, that the sorrow passes by us: the new thing in us, that has been added to us, has entered into our heart, has gone into its innermost chamber, and is no more even there,—is already in the blood. And we do not realize what it was. We could easily be made to believe that nothing had happened, and yet we have been changed, as a house is changed into which a guest has entered. We cannot say who has come, perhaps we shall never know, but there are many indications to suggest that the future is entering into us in this manner in order to transform itself within us long before it happens. And therefore it is so important to be solitary and heedful when we are sad: because the seemingly uneventful and inflexible moment when our future sets foot in us stands so much nearer to life than that other noisy and fortuitous instant when it happens to us as if from without. The more patient, quiet and open we are in our sorrowing, the more deeply and the more unhesitatingly will the new thing enter us, the better shall we deserve it, the more will it be our own destiny, and when one day later it "happens" (that is, goes forth from us to others) we shall feel in our inmost selves that we are akin and close to it. And that is necessary. It is necessary—and in that direction our development will gradually move—, that nothing alien shall befall us,

36

but only what has long been part of us. We have already had to think anew so many concepts of motion, we shall also learn gradually to realize that it is out of mankind that what we call destiny proceeds, not into them from without. Only because so many did not absorb their destinies and transform these within themselves as long as they lived in them, they did not recognize what went forth from them; it was so alien to them that they believed, in their bewildered terror, it must have just entered into them, for they swore that they had never before found anything similar in themselves. As we have long deceived ourselves about the motion of the sun, so we still continue to deceive ourselves about the motion of that which is to come. The future stands firm, dear Herr Kappus, but we move about in infinite space.

How should we not find it difficult?

And, to speak again of solitude, it becomes increasingly clear that this is fundamentally not something that we can choose or reject. We *are* solitary. We can delude ourselves about it, and pretend that it is not so. That is all. But how much better it is to realize that we are thus, to start directly from that very point. Then, to be sure, it will come about that we grow dizzy; for all the points upon which our eyes have been accustomed to rest will be taken away from us, there is no longer any nearness, and all distance is infinitely far. A man who was taken from his study, almost without preparation and transition, and placed upon the height of a great mountain range, would be bound to feel something similar: an uncertainty without parallel, an abandonment to the unutterable would almost annihilate him. He would imagine himself to be falling or fancy himself flung outwards into space or exploded into a thousand pieces: what a monstrous lie his brain would have to invent in order to retrieve and explain the condition of his senses. So all distances, all measures are changed for the man who becomes solitary; many of these changes take effect suddenly, and, as with the man on the mountain top, there arise singular fantasies and strange sensations which seem to grow out beyond all endurance.

But it is necessary for us to experience that too. We must accept our existence as far as ever it is possible; everything, even the unheard of, must be possible there. That is fundamentally the only courage which is demanded of us: to be brave in the face of the strangest, most singular and most inexplicable things that can befall us. The fact that human beings have been cowardly in this sense has done endless harm to life; the experiences that are called "apparitions", the whole of the so-called "spirit world", death, all these things that are so closely related to us, have been so crowded out of life by our daily warding them off, that the senses by which we might apprehend them are stunted. To say nothing of God. But fear of the inexplicable has not only impoverished the existence of the solitary man, it has also circumscribed the relationships between human beings, as it were lifted them up from the river bed of infinite possibilities to a fallow spot on the bank, to which nothing happens. For it is not only indolence which causes human relationships to repeat themselves with such unspeakable monotony, unrenewed from one occasion to another, it is the shyness of any new, incalculable experience which we do not feel ourselves equal to facing. But only the man who is prepared for everything, who excludes nothing, not even the most unintelligible, will live the relationship with another as something vital, and will himself exhaust his own existence. For if we think of this existence of the individual as a larger or smaller room, it becomes clear that most people get to know only one corner of their room, a window seat, a strip of floor which they pace up and down. In that way they have a certain security. And yet how much more human is that insecurity, so fraught with danger, which compels the prisoners in Poe's Tales to grope for the shapes of their ghastly prisons and not to remain unaware of the unspeakable horrors of their dwelling. But we are not prisoners. No snares and springes are laid for us, and there is nothing that should alarm or torment us. We are set in life as in the element with which we are most in keeping, and we have moreover, through thousands of years of adaptation, become so similar to this life that when we stay still we are, by a happy mimicry, hardly to be distinguished from our surroundings. We have no cause to be mistrustful of our world, for it is not against us. If it has terrors they are our terrors; if it has abysses those abysses belong to us, if dangers are there we must strive to love them. And if only we regulate our life according to that principle which advises us always to hold to the difficult, what even now appears most alien to us will become most familiar and loyal. How could we forget those old myths which are to be found in the beginnings of every people; the myths of the dragons which are transformed, at the last moment, into princesses; perhaps all the dragons of our life are princesses, who are only waiting to see us once beautiful and brave. Perhaps everything terrifying is at bottom the helplessness that seeks our help.

So you must not be frightened, dear Herr Kappus, when a sorrow rises up before you, greater than you have ever seen before; when a restlessness like light and cloud shadows passes over your hands and over all your doing. You must think that something is happening upon you, that life has not forgotten you, that it holds you in its hand; it will not let you fall. Why do you want to exclude any disturbance, any pain, any melancholy from your life, since you do not know what these conditions are working upon you? Why do you want to plague yourself with the question where it has all come from and whither it is tending? Since you know that you are in a state of transition and would wish nothing so dearly as to transform yourself. If something in your proceedings is diseased, do reflect that disease is the means by which an organism rids itself of a foreign body; you must then simply help it to be ill, to have its full disease and to let it break out, for that is its development. In you, dear Herr Kappus, so much is happening now; you must be patient like a sick man and sanguine like a convalescent; for perhaps you are both. And more than that: you are also the doctor who has to superintend yourself. But in every illness there are many days when the doctor can do nothing but wait. And that is what you, in so far as you are your own doctor, must now above all things do.

Do not observe yourself too closely. Do not draw too rapid conclusions from what happens to you; let it simply happen to you. Otherwise you will too easily reach the point of looking reproachfully (that is morally) at your past, which is naturally concerned with everything that is now occurring to you. But what is taking effect in you from the mistakes, desires and longings of your boyhood is not what you recall and condemn. The extraordinary circumstances of a solitary and helpless childhood are so difficult, so complicated, exposed to so many influences and at the same time so untrammelled by all real connection with life, that where a vice appears in it we must not call it a vice and leave it at that. One must in general be so careful with names; it is so often the name of a misdeed upon which a life is shattered, not the nameless and personal action itself, which was perhaps a quite definite necessity of that life and could be taken on by it without trouble. And the expense of energy seems to you so great only because you overrate the victory; this latter is not the "great thing" that you think you have achieved, although you are right about your feeling; the great thing is that something was already there which you could set in place of that betrayal, something true and genuine. Apart from this even your victory would have been only a moral reaction without great significance, but thus it has become a chapter of your life. Of your life, dear Herr Kappus, about which I am thinking with so many wishes. Do you remember how this life has longed ever since childhood for the "great"? I see how it is now longing to leave the great for greater. Therefore it does not cease to be difficult, but therefore it will not cease, either, to grow.

And if I may say one thing more to you, it is this: do not think that the man who seeks to comfort you lives untroubled among the simple and quiet words which sometimes do you good. His life has much hardship and sadness and lags far behind you. If it were otherwise, he could never have found those words.

Yours :

RAINER MARIA RILKE.

IX

FURUBORG,[22] JONSERED, SWEDEN, November 4th 1904.

MY DEAR HERR KAPPUS,

during the time which has passed without a letter I have been partly on the move, partly so busy that I could not write. And even today I find writing difficult, because I have already had to write a number of letters, so that my hand is tired. If I could dictate, I would say much to you, but as it is you must accept only a few words in answer to your long letter.

I think of you often, dear Herr Kappus, and with such concentrated wishes that it really must help you in some way. Whether my letters could be truly a help, I often doubt. Do not say : yes, they are. Accept them quietly and without many thanks, and let us wait to see what will come.

It is perhaps no use now to reply to your actual words ; for what I could say about your disposition to doubt or about your inability to bring your outer and inner life into harmony, or about anything else that oppresses you— : it is always what I have said before : always the wish that you might be able to find patience enough in yourself to endure, and single-heartedness enough to believe ; that you might win increasing trust in what is difficult, and in your solitude among other people. And for the rest, let life happen to you. Believe me : life is right, at all events.

And about feelings : all feelings are pure which gather you

41

and lift you up; a feeling is impure which takes hold of only one side of your being and so distorts you. Everything that you could think in the light of your childhood is good. Everything which makes more of you than you have previously been in your best hours, is right. Every exaltation is good if it is in your whole blood, if it is not intoxication or turbidness, but joy into whose depths you can see. Do you understand what I mean?

And your doubt can become a good quality if you train it. It must become *aware*, it must become criticism. Ask it, whenever it wants to spoil something for you, *why* something is ugly, demand proofs from it, test it, and you will perhaps find it helpless and nonplussed, perhaps also aggressive. But do not give way, demand arguments and conduct yourself thus carefully and consistently every single time, and the day will dawn when it will become, instead of a subverter, one of your best workmen,—perhaps the cleverest of all who are building at your life.

That is all, dear Herr Kappus, that I am able to say to you today. But I am sending you by the same post the off-print of a little composition [23] which has just appeared in the Prague *Deutsche Arbeit*. There I speak to you further of life and of death, and of the greatness and splendour of both.

Yours:

RAINER MARIA RILKE.

X

PARIS,[24] *the second day of Christmas* 1908.

You must know, dear Herr Kappus, how glad I was to have that beautiful letter from you. The news which you give me, real and expressible as it now again is, seems to me good, and the longer I have considered it, the more I have felt that it is in actual fact good. I really wanted to write this to you for Christmas Eve; but with all the work in which I have been variously and unremittingly living this winter, the festival has come upon me so quickly that I have hardly had any time over to see to my most necessary business, much less to write.

But I have thought of you often during these festival days, and imagined how quiet you must be in your lonely fort among the empty mountains, over which those great southerly winds are pouring themselves as if they wanted to devour them in great lumps.

The stillness must be immense in which such sounds and movements have room, and when one considers that to all these is added at the same time the resounding presence of the distant sea, perhaps as the innermost voice in this prehistoric harmony, one can only wish for you that you may confidently and patiently let that sublime solitude work upon you, which can no more be expunged from your life; which will work continuously and with gentle decision as an anonymous influence in everything that lies before you, somewhat as ancestral blood moves incessantly within us and mingles with our own to form that unique and unrepeatable compound that we are at every turning of our life.

Yes: I am glad that you have this steady expressible existence with you, this title, this uniform, this duty, all this which is palpable and defined, which in such surroundings with a similarly isolated, not numerous body of men assumes gravity and necessity, betokens a vigilant employment over and above that element of playing and passing the time in the military profession, and not only admits but positively trains an independent alertness. And that we are in circumstances which work upon us, which set us free from time to time to face things that are great and natural, is all that is necessary.

Art too is only a way of living, and one can prepare for it, living somehow, without knowing it; in everything real one is a closer, nearer neighbour to it than in the unreal semi-artistic professions which, while they make show of a relatedness to art, in practice deny and attack the existence of all art, as for instance the whole of journalism does, and almost all criticism and three-quarters of what calls itself and likes to be called literature. I am glad, in a word, that you have overcome the danger of ending up there,[25] and remain solitary and courageous somewhere in a raw reality. May the year that lies before you preserve and strengthen you in that.

Ever yours:

R. M. Rilke.

COMMENTARY

NOTE I, PAGE 8

The issue of the *Inselschiff* devoted to Rilke's memory contains replicas of his handwriting at six different stages in his career, from *Cornet* to the tenth *Duinese Elegy*. His early hand is most beautiful: the letters are small but perfectly formed, and the paragraphs and spacing are judged with a painter's eye.

NOTE 2, PAGE II

Rilke is not politely evading the necessity for saying something unkind: he often expressed his distaste for aesthetic criticism, and avowed that he took no notice of printed opinions about his own works (though there is some evidence that he was sensitive when he saw them, as he did more often than pure accident can be held accountable for). Once when his friend the philosopher Kassner reproached him with his indulgence towards a piece of writing, he said "very excitedly" that he never wanted to criticize, that it signified nothing to him. Kassner continues: "In truth he had not this masculine separation between judgment and feeling that belongs so peculiarly to man. Oh, he took absolutely no cognizance of man. Man remained an intruder in Rilke's world; only children, women and old people were at home in it" (*Inselschiff*, April 1927, p. 120). Earlier on he had written: "I must be alone with my work, and have as little need of hearing others talk of it as a man might wish to see in print, and to collect, others' opinions about the woman he loves" (*Letters 1906-1907*, p. 318).

NOTE 3, PAGE 12

If Goethe's dictum be true, that "he is the most fortunate of men who can trace an unbroken connection between the end of his life and the beginning", Rilke was blessed indeed. He himself told his son-in-law and biographer that the roots of his life's work went back far into his childhood. Rilke's life was peculiarly of a piece, a coat without seam; nothing that enriched his last great poems was not discernible, in rudimentary form, in his earliest writing, and not one of the essentials of his youthful character and genius appears to have become atrophied in him. At the age of thirty-five he was still re-living his own childhood, with fascination and with anguish, in the wonderful childhood passages of *Malte Laurids Brigge*; and his fourth *Duinese Elegy*, written in the bitter war years, looks to the integrity of childhood as the only resolution of the fatal dichotomy between the actual and the possible in human nature, and to its timelessness as the only answer to the challenge of time.

NOTE 4, PAGE 14

After seven months of living in Paris, exhausted by ill-health and the power of Rodin's personality, Rilke could bear his imprisonment in this city of hospitals, "armies of sick, hosts of dying, nations of dead" no more, and fled alone to a favourite haunt * in Italy for some weeks of solitude and sun-bathing. He lay in the warm sand, ran and danced in the wind, swam in the sea, and loved whenever possible to cast off his borrowed bathing-costume of red-and-black striped stockinette and take these pleasures naked. This was the beach where Shelley's body was washed ashore and buried, later to be exhumed and burned.

NOTE 5, PAGE 15

Jens Peter Jacobsen (1847-1885), naturalist and psychological novelist, was the son of a merchant and a schoolmaster's daughter, who gave him a happy upbringing in a little harbour town in Denmark. The enthusiasm of his youth was divided between botany (his expeditions in the near-by marshes in search of algae possibly undermined his health) and versifying (his early poems were damned with faint praise by the great critic Georg

---

* In that same year Viareggio was harbouring two other holiday-makers, d'Annunzio and Ouida.

Brandes). He had first gone to school at the age of four, and completed his studies at the University of Copenhagen, where he learnt to know the work of Darwin, whom he introduced to his countrymen in a series of articles. In the course of time he translated *The Origin of Species* and *The Descent of Man* into Danish. He lost the firm religious faith of his boyhood, and constructed for himself a "natural" religion based on the new biology and the "poetry of science"; a romanticist at heart, he rejected all supernatural romantic existences, and, an objectively minded scientist, sought for spiritual satisfaction in the beauty of the natural world. He travelled in Germany, Bohemia, Austria and Italy, and at Florence, when he was twenty-six years old, consumption declared itself in such a violent form that his doctors gave Jacobsen a bare two years to live. He actually had eleven years ahead of him, of life carefully tended and interrupted by frequent ill health.

His first and best short story, *Mogens*, had been published when he was twenty-four, and he now set to work on a historical novel, *Maria Grubbe*, which was published when he was twenty-nine, and extremely well received. Its outspokenness was considered shocking by a public that had yet to read Ibsen's *Ghosts* and Strindberg's stories, which appeared later in the same decade. Four years after *Maria Grubbe* he published *Niels Lyhne*, a study of emotional decadence, the story of the conflict in a young would-be poet between his inner dream world and the outer realities of life. The appearance of this book was as perfectly timed by the *Zeitgeist* as that of *Werther* had been, and it was the forerunner and pattern of much of the decadent literature on the Continent during the 'nineties. It discussed ideas—mainly the struggle between romanticism and positivism for the heart of contemporary youth—in a kind of hot-house haze. As a study of the disintegration of character that proceeds from weak romantic illusion, objectively and mercilessly written, it has been likened to *Madame Bovary*; but Lyhne's neurosis is of the intellect, not of the heart, and it would in any case be absurd to compare Jacobsen with Flaubert as a creative artist. The conventional unconventionality of Jacobsen's religious attitude, a species of *fin-de-siècle* humanism, born of materialistic physics

47

and nourished on sensuous emotionalism, and his battle-cry (if one can speak of anything so energetic and direct as a battle in connection with this subtle, world-weary, gently ironical writer) —his challenge "There is no God, and Man is his prophet" naturally endeared him to the rebellious young, and the book became the Bible of the growing poets and painters of the day. As a piece of literary history it is certainly important, and a critic so little *schwärmerisch* as Ibsen solemnly declared it to be the best book of the century. Jacobsen died in his native town at the age of thirty-eight, just as little René Rilke was being sent off to school.

It was the novelist Jakob Wassermann who first recommended Jacobsen to the poet, then in his early twenties, and the effect on him was immediate, profound, and lasting. He read the novels and tales in German translation, and his prose style clearly owes much to his literary idol. But it was not only the fastidious choice of words and the artistic purity and integrity of the Danish writer that appealed to Rilke; it was not only that the two men were trying to solve the same aesthetic problem—the combination of accurate, objective, almost plastic solidity of description with complete freedom from the *clichés* of conventional realism; the germs of some of Rilke's most important ideas are to be found in Jacobsen's books, in particular those of solitude and of "personal" death (though Lou Andreas-Salomé, in her memoir of Rilke, maintains that it was the death by apoplexy of an uncle that gave rise to his "childish fantasy" of the private death). Just before she died, Maria Grubbe had said that "everyone lives his own life and dies his own death"; and the concluding words of *Niels Lyhne* are "at last he died his death, his difficult death"— a phrase which bore fruit in the superb deathbed description at the beginning of *Malte Laurids Brigge*.

It is impossible to regard Rilke's estimate of Jacobsen to young Kappus as a balanced literary judgment: Jacobsen's talent was real, but not finally important. Yet it was of seminal importance for Rilke himself, and for his artistic development; nor was it a transient enthusiasm—fifteen years later we find him recommending *Niels Lyhne* to correspondents, known and unknown, with the warmth of his approval undiminished. Jacobsen was a pioneer of the "stream of consciousness" novel of today, and his handling of the subconscious life is masterly. A strong biological sense runs through *Niels Lyhne*, and as a study in heredity alone it is first-rate. Brandes has compared Jacobsen with Correggio, and credits him with a consummate artistry that just falls short of affectation and morbidity.

[The two novels have appeared in America, *Maria Grubbe* in 1914 and *Niels Lyhne* in 1919, both translated by H. A. Larsen and published by the American-Scandinavian Foundation. In England there are published a single short story, *The Plague in Bergamo*, tr. E. Ellefsen (Porpoise Press, 1923), and *Poems*, tr. P. Selver (Oxford, 1920).]

NOTE 6, PAGE 16

Rilke had already written the first part of his Rodin book, and was probably glad to have a holiday from the influence of the older man (when he went to Paris Rilke was twenty-seven and Rodin sixty-two years old), who inspired and exhausted him at the same time. His influence was mainly maieutic, and he helped the poet to learn two valuable lessons : how to work and how to see. Before Clara joined him in Paris in the autumn of 1902, Rilke had described to her how the sculptor had agreed with him about solitude. He quotes Rodin as saying : "Il n'est pas bien de faire des groupes, les amis s'empêchent. Il est mieux d'être seul. Peut-être avoir une femme—parce qu'il faut avoir une femme." Solitude made possible real work, and "il faut travailler, rien que travailler. Et il faut avoir patience" (*Letters 1902-1906*, p. 36). "Tolstoy's uncomfortable household," he goes on in the same letter—for he had paid a short and slightly embarrassing visit to the grim old man at Yasnaya Polyana—"the lack of ease in Rodin's rooms : it all points to the same thing : that one must decide, either this or that. Either happiness or art. On doit trouver le bonheur dans son art. . . . Rodin said something of that kind too. And indeed it is all so clear, so clear. All great men have let their life become overgrown like an old path and have carried everything into their art. Their life is atrophied like an organ that they no more use. . . ." Rilke had always known the meaning of the work "that gives everything if one believes in it and demands everything from it"; when he was only twenty-four he had said: "my work remains the highest court of appeal, and before the glance of a bestowing hour all ordinary duties must be dumb" (*Letters 1899-1902*, p. 10).

Rodin also helped the poet to look at things, or rather to *see* things. "What he sees and surrounds with sight is always to him the only thing, the world in which everything is happening; when he moulds a hand, it is alone in space, and nothing exists but a hand; and God in six days made only a hand and poured out the waters round it and arched the heavens above it; and rested upon it when all was completed, and there was a glory and a hand" (quoted by Lou Andreas-Salomé in her *Memoirs*, p. 36). Rodin was but confirming what the poet had already in part learnt from Jacobsen, Cézanne and others: to concentrate on the object (to Rilke always the Thing) rather than on his feelings about that object, not to wrestle with it as Jacob wrestled with the angel, until he should force it to tell its name and so yield its secret power, but to wait upon it with infinite patience and concentration, to gaze at—or rather into—it as Blake gazed at his knot of wood, "until it hurt". Readers of *Malte* will recall the saying: "He was a poet and hated the approximate."

NOTE 7, PAGE 16

Since writing the previous letter Rilke had been full of creative activity: the "bestowing hour" came to him and within a single week in April he wrote the whole of the third part of the *Book of Hours*, the *Book of Poverty and Death* in which his horror of Paris finds release in poetry.

NOTE 8, PAGE 17

This is one of the shortest and slightest of Jacobsen's *Six Tales*, a little reminiscent of Oscar Wilde's fairy stories.

NOTE 9, PAGE 18

Richard Dehmel (1863-1920) was a poet of vigour and real creative genius, neither of which was under adequate control.

Rilke was certainly influenced by him, probably for the good, in his twenties, and speaks of Dehmel's name as a "hard and significant" one for his own artistic development. *Deliverances, But Love, Woman and World* are three revealing titles of his books of lyrics, and he wrote a novel in lyrical form and several dramas and pantomimes. His themes are erotic, social and purely lyrical, the first being on the whole the most tasteless, the second the most sincere, and the third the most artistically successful. He was keenly concerned with sexual social problems, and at one time was drawn into the literary orbit of Dostoevsky and the cult of the holy whore. In the European War he volunteered for the German army at the age of over fifty, and a contemporary photograph of him shews a fierce, proud-nostrilled face with eyes gleaming balefully from beneath his *Pickelhaube*—a perfect type of what Coleridge called Teutonic nimiety.

NOTE 10, PAGE 20

Rilke had returned to Paris, after his month in Italy, with his health scarcely improved. He decided to spend the whole summer of 1903 recuperating in Germany, at Worpswede and Ober-neuland near by; and this time Clara accompanied him. A remarkable letter which he wrote shortly after his arrival at Worpswede (much of it was later lifted bodily into the pages of *Malte Laurids Brigge*) shewed that he had not yet come to terms with his dread of great cities. "The carriages drove right through me, and hurrying people did not swerve aside for me and ran over me full of contempt, as over a bad place in which stale water has collected. . . . O what a world it is! Pieces, pieces of people, parts of animals, remains of finished things, and everything still on the move, driving about as if in an uncanny wind, carried and carrying, falling and catching themselves up in their fall" (*Letters 1902-1906*, pp. 98-9).

NOTE 11, PAGE 21

"Omnia praeclara tam difficilia quam rara sunt"—Spinoza, the philosopher of poets from Lessing, Goethe, Coleridge, Wordsworth and Shelley onwards.

NOTE 12, PAGE 23

It is time to speak of Rilke's conception of solitude in a little detail. He himself refers to it as his "solitude fanaticism". Perhaps he first knew it as the sheer apartness of his boyhood, this "boy who liked to keep himself apart" as Horaček described him; it was then solitude into which one escaped from the cruelty of one's fellows. But even at that time he saw more in solitude than that: it meant the possibility of meeting God. "If God has given a commandment, it is this: Be solitary from time to time. For he can come only to one man, or to two whom he can no longer distinguish" (*Journal* Nov. 25th 1899). In solitude, too, one might learn to understand things, and draw near to them. "Have you never yet noticed how despised and insignificant things come to themselves if they fall into the ready, tender hands of a solitary? They are like little birds to whom warmth returns, they bestir themselves, awaken, and a heart begins to beat in them, that rises and falls like the uttermost wave of a mighty ocean in the hearkening hands" (*Journal* Dec. 3rd-4th 1899). Solitude was not arrived at numerically, but qualitatively—"Friends do not prevent our solitude, they only limit our aloneness" (*Journal* Sept. 15th 1900). Real solitude might bring a rich reward: "To the solitary there comes from time to time something wonderfully beneficent. It is no sound, no splendour, and also no voice. It is the smile of women who have passed away, which, like the light of dead stars, is still on its way to us" (*Journal* Sept. 13th 1900). Only in solitude could real seeing be practised: "To everyone that gazes there comes some time the longing to go into the wilderness. With little nourishment, to sit upon a stone and to think difficult thoughts, so difficult that they lie heavy on the eyelids. But so far all have returned from the wilderness to those that once they left. And they have wanted to teach solitude to the companionable; thus they grew tired, despaired of themselves and died the little torturing death. But we must go out across the wilderness, further, ever in one direction. Only one who succeeds in doing that will know what lies beyond solitude and why we seek the wilderness" (*Journal* April 7th 1900).

When Rilke went to Russia, the land that "borders on God",

he found that solitude was filled with the presence of God, and it became more than ever a necessity for him. His very marriage he regarded as an assurance of solitude; soon after he set up house at Westerwede he wrote to Paula Becker: "I hold this to be the highest task for a union of two people: that one shall guard the other's solitude. For if it is the nature of indifference and of the multitude to acknowledge no solitude, love and friendship exists to give continually opportunity for solitude. The only real communions are those which interrupt rhythmically profound solitude" (*Letters 1899-1902*, p. 167).

If he appreciated the value of extraordinary solitude as few artists have done, it is possible that he underrated the value of ordinary communion; he enjoyed it well enough when it came his way, and sometimes felt an almost morbid craving for it, but it exhausted him. "Among people, particularly those I love, I so easily get talking and give out everything possible in conversation, so that it is not available for my work. It is a stupid piece of clumsiness that I am so wanting in the gift of sociability, the talent for easy but at the same time recreative conversations, in which one does not exert and expend oneself" (*Letters 1906-1907*, p. 118).

NOTE 13, PAGE 24

The whole of the late autumn and winter of 1903, and the spring of the following year, Rilke spent in Rome, greatly perplexed about his art, feeling that he had not yet begun to write, doubting his own ability as a craftsman in comparison with Rodin (with whom he had broken). It was at Rome that he began to write his *Malte Laurids Brigge*, which was not finished for another seven years.

NOTE 14, PAGE 26

The word that Rilke uses to describe the lodging is *Altan*, which signifies a high balcony. It was in point of fact "a little red building on the arch of a bridge spanning the main pathway of the garden [of a villa] ... built years ago as a summer house, it contains a single simple high windowed room and carries a flat roof, from which one sees the Roman landscape afar"

(*Letters 1902-1906*, p. 131). It was not the only queer habitation that the poet was to know, until his last days in a tiny Swiss castle. Clara, whom Rodin had advised to study in Rome, had lodgings and a studio in the same gardens, and the two occasionally met. Rilke later referred to himself as having been "alone, with no one in the neighbourhood but my wife, who was also working, so that we didn't see each other as often as once a day, and yet were helping one another" (*Letters 1902-1906*, pp. 308-9).

NOTE 15, PAGE 27

Rilke had written of Jacobsen that he "had no experience, no love, no adventure and no wisdom, only a childhood. A great, immensely coloured childhood in which he found everything that his soul needed in order to disguise itself fantastically" (*Journal* Sept. 29th 1900).

NOTE 16, PAGE 28

Perhaps Thing should carry a capital letter, for it meant to Rilke much more than an object. A full exegesis is impossible here; it must be sufficient to say that *Dinge* have a long and respectable ancestry in German literature, as indeed in European philosophy generally. This notion of the visible as somehow a paradigm of the invisible is as old as Plato, though Rilke would have energetically repudiated any form of philosophical idealism, in which he was as little interested, and as ill read, as Goethe. (Purely as an artist, it appears that he never appreciated that greatest of Germans—he himself said that he "lacked the receptive organ for Goethe", and, incredible as it may seem, he had never read *Faust*, though he came to understand and revere the hieratic art of one who is at least Goethe's peer, and possibly his superior, simply as a poet—Friedrich Hölderlin, whom oddly he did not discover till his fortieth year.) One of the letters from Rome runs: "You know what the presence of things says to me; and I am the whole day in conversation with things. . . . My practice of seeing and reading from things as they are, my faithfulness in letting my eyes be my light, my total repudiation of all pretension, are standing me in good stead once again. . . ." This was written not by Rilke, but by Goethe more than a century before him (*Italian Journey* Nov. 1786); and Albrecht Dürer had said Rilkean things about humility before the object, two hundred years even before that. Schiller describes Nature as "voluntary being, the arising of things by themselves, their existence according to their individual and immutable laws. . . . What we love in them is the quiet creative life, the gentle working out of themselves, the subsistence according to their own laws, the inner necessity, the eternal oneness with themselves. They are what we were; they are what we are again to become. . . . They are therefore at the same time delineation of our lost childhood, which remains eternally the most precious thing to us; therefore they fill us with a certain melancholy. They are also delineations of our highest completion in the ideal, therefore they exalt us to a sublime emotion" (*On Naïve and Sentimental Poetry*). In the middle of the nineteenth century Mörike was attempting to solve, in his "thing poems", exactly the problem that faced Rilke when he was writing the *Book of Images*.

The first stage, for Rilke, was the simple experiencing of Things, through love and patience; the poet speaks quietly about things, rather than listens to their secret. Later this subjective approach yields to pure objectivity; the accidents of the Things fall away, the substance stands revealed as pure Being, a hypostatic realization of the unutterable. The task of the artist, in Rilke's view, was so to transform the visible into the invisible, the outward into the inward, that he would finally himself become world. The Things that began by needing human deliverance, now support and nourish mankind; they mediate between man and not-man, and help the artist not indeed to see the beatific vision, but (to anticipate for one moment a discussion of Rilke's theology) to create it, to work upon God. Thus Things speak to man of God. In Martin Buber's phrase the *I-It* has given place, for ever, to the *I-Thou*. There are features of this private poetic gnosticism which recall some of the less orthodox descriptions of the mystic scale, as well as the stages prescribed by Diotima (Plato's, not Hölderlin's) for the ascent of love. In the third and final stage, the distinction between Thing and poet appears to have broken down, and by a species of divine anastomosis knower and known interfuse and are one. Rilke came finally to believe that he had achieved a large measure of this transformation, and could write: "Very seldom now, and as if inadvertently, does a Thing address me vouchsafingly and givingly, without an equivalent and significant demand being called out in myself." Of the Spanish landscape—"the last that I boundlessly experienced"—he said that "everywhere appearance and vision came, as it were, together in the object, there was in each one a whole inner world revealed, as though an angel who encloses space were blind and gazing into himself" (*Letters 1914-1921*, p. 80). So art, which began by exploring Nature in search of an object to "gaze" upon, ends in rejection of the physical world: "I believe no one has experienced more distinctly the extent to which art goes against Nature, it is the most passionate inversion of the world, the road back from the Infinite, on which we meet all true Things, now we see them in their wholeness, their face draws near, their motion attains individuality—: yes, but who are we that we may tread this road, that we may take this direction in the face of them all, this everlasting turning round by which we deceive them, letting them think we had already arrived somewhere at some goal, and now had leisure to come back?" (*Letters 1907-1914*, p. 111). The closing note of humility is characteristic.

NOTE 17, PAGE 29

Just as Kierkegaard's father, in his desire to impress his child with the sufferings of Christ, slipped in among his toys a picture of the Crucifixion, so Rilke's mother taught him to kiss the nail-marks in the figure on the crucifix. As a result, one boy learnt to love and revere, the other to loathe and fear, the human sufferings of the Saviour. Like Goethe, Rilke grew up in rebellion against the Christian creed, but unlike the great poet who did not dare to look at a coffin, he early came to terms with death, and held it to be one of man's chief duties to "hold life open towards death". He believed at all times, as Goethe had done, that the ethical teaching of Christ was the only pattern for human beings and human society to follow; like him, he was constantly inspired and helped by the Bible; and like him, he violently rejected all Christian doctrine. There is a great deal about God (and very little about the person of Christ) in Rilke's early poetry and prose, but it is impossible to reduce all his sayings to a definite system, though the attempt has often been made by the poet's German hagiographers. It is poet's theology, not the real thing; only once has theology other than the crudest sort been successfully combined with true poetry without mutual injury. Rilke's was an *anima naturaliter religiosa*, and the whole of his art may be regarded as an effort towards religious expression. His religion has nothing like the purity of Kierkegaard's, and sinks at times to religiosity; but there is no question of his whole-hearted longing to "glorify God and to enjoy him for ever".

Rilke was officially a Roman Catholic until about the age of eighteen, but by his early twenties the main lines of his later religious development were laid down: in his Tuscan Journal he declared the Christian God to be "dead, the oldest work of art and very badly preserved", and entirely denied God's existence except as artists created him. In Russia he was confirmed in this view of God as Becoming, God "with nothing final about him, always growing and being transformed", and the *Book of Monkish Life* illustrates his early struggles to express this belief. The metaphor of man as a workman upon the slowly growing cathedral of God runs right through this first part of the *Book of Hours*, and is expressed in a variety of ways with great beauty and humility. He recalls a conversation about God at Worpswede, after his return from Russia, when "I gently spoke of Him. That his defects, his injustice and everything inadequate about his power lay in his development. That he was not completed. When was he supposed to have ever *become*? Man needed Him so urgently that he experienced and saw Him right from the start as existing. Man needed him ready made, and he said: God is. Now he must catch up with his becoming. And it is we who help him to do that. With us he *becomes*, with our joys he grows, and our Sorrows begin to form the shadows in his countenance. We can do nothing that is not done upon Him, when we have once found ourselves. And you must not think of Him as over the crowd. Crowd was not his intention, he wanted to be borne by many individuals. In the crowd each one is so small that he cannot lay hands upon the building of God. But the individual who advances towards Him gazes into his countenance and reaches certainly up to his shoulder. And is mighty in face of Him. And is important for God. And this it is which best buoys me up : that I must be great in order to benefit his greatness, that I must be simple in order not to confuse Him, and that my being solemn somewhere borders on his solemnity . . ." (*Journal* Oct. 4th 1900). A thoroughly Kierkegaardian feature of Rilke's religious thought was his passionate denial of the easy accessibility of God : " O ye men, when they bring you God, the good docile dogs who have fetched him at risk of their lives, then take him and fling him out again into immensity. For God *is not* to be brought to the shore by the good docile dogs. He is not in danger upon his surging waters, and a great wave that is still to come will lift him on to the land which is worthy of him" (*Journal* March 1901). His son-in-law Carl Sieber says that what particularly repelled him was the notion that "we carry God about with us like small change" (Introduction to *Two Letters about God*). Sieber goes on to quote Rilke's answer to a query of Ellen Key in 1904, that after the difficult experiences of his life he had come to believe that those people were right who felt and said at a certain period of development of their spirit that there was no God and never could have been one. "But", said Rilke, "this recognition is something *infinitely affirmative* for me, for now all fear that he might be used up and perished is removed from me, now I know *that he will be*. He will be, and those who are solitary and withdraw from time are building him, building him with their heart, their head and their hands . . ." (*op. cit., loc. cit.*).

Rilke has often been termed a mystic, and though Keyserling always insisted that he was nothing of the kind, there is much in the *Book of Hours* that finds a close parallel in other writers of the German mystical tradition. The poem beginning "What wilt thou do, God, if I die ?" recalls Angelus Silesius' "I know that without me God cannot live an instant", and Meister Eckhart's paradox "God needs me as much as I need him", as well as the Lady Julian's lovely saying that "We are God's bliss, for in us

He enjoyeth without end". Parallel passages may easily be found in the writings of Tauler and St John of the Cross. That great mystical utterance, the final lyric of the second part of *Faust*, has expressed perfectly, and for ever, the hopelessness of the poet's task in striving to express the Beyond in terms of the Here. Elsewhere Goethe had written: "The highest, the most excellent thing in man is . . . without form, and we should guard against representing it otherwise than in noble action" (*Elective Affinities*, Pt. II, ch. 7). Rilke was a natural worshipper, and in places came near to sharing Goethe's view that "the finest achievement for a thinker is to have fathomed what may be fathomed, and quietly to adore the unfathomable". The mystics are mostly sublime stammerers, and their descriptions must be mainly negative; absolute mysticism precludes artistic expression absolutely. Rilke tried in the *Book of Hours* to express God in an infinite variety of terms, and he swings from complete transcendence to complete immanence. At one time God seems to be only the "dark", the "mysterious", the "subtle"; then suddenly he is the "Neighbour God", nearer indeed than neighbour—closer to us, as Mohammed used to say, than our jugular vein. But in later years "you would hardly ever hear me name him, there exists an indescribable discretion between us, and where once was nearness and permeation, are stretched new distances, as in the atom, which modern science also conceives as a universe in microcosm" (*Letters 1921-1926*, pp. 95-6). Finally, God seems to withdraw entirely from the Here, and to belong only to the Beyond; he becomes *totaliter aliter*, and Rilke looks upon him as a being that does not return our love (here he was carrying on the tradition of Spinoza's "Qui deum amat, conari non potest, ut Deus ipsum contra amet", and the words that Goethe puts into the mouth of his Philine, "If I love thee, what is that to thee?").

Rilke had no sympathy for, and seemingly no understanding of, the notions of original sin, sacrifice and redemption. "Religion is something infinitely simple, simple-minded! It is no knowledge, no content of feeling, it is no duty and no renunciation, it is no limitation: but in the entire expanse of the universe it is: a direction of the heart" (*Letters 1921-1926*, p. 65). He rejected the idea of mediation, and told Kassner that "Christ was in his way". "The notion of our being sinful and needing redemption as the presupposition of our finding God is increasingly repugnant to a heart that has comprehended the earth. It is not sinfulness and earthly error, but on the contrary man's pure nature that grows into essential consciousness; sin is certainly the most wonderful détour to God,—but why should they go on their wanderings who have never left him? The strong, inwardly quivering bridge of the mediator has meaning only where the gulf between God and ourselves is admitted—, but this very gulf is full of the darkness of God, and where a man experiences it let him climb down and howl there (that is more necessary than crossing it). It is the man who had even the gulf as his dwelling place that the heavens, which were always potentially his, will turn to meet, and to him will return everything deep and inwardly belonging to the Here, which the Church has fraudulently converted to the Beyond; all the angels decide, in songs of praise, for earth" (*Letters 1921-1926*, p. 186). He was not interested in eschatology. He rejected earthly renunciation for the sake of heavenly reward, himself preaching, and practising, a life that was neither ascetic nor apolaustic. He disliked what he conceived to be the Catholic denigration of this world as a mere ancillary of the world to come; he believed it to be man's task to transform and above all to praise this world— a task which he personally performed with humility, pertinacity and an almost Hegelian justification of the thing which is. "Since my productiveness proceeds in the final analysis from the most immediate admiration of life, from the daily inexhaustible amazement at it (how else should I have come to create?), I should regard it as a lie to refuse even for a moment its flow towards me; every such denial must in the end find expression as hardness within the sphere of art itself, and so bring its revenge, however much that art may gain potentially thereby; for who could be quite open and consenting in so sensitive a sphere, if he has a distrustful, reserved and uneasy attitude towards life!" (*Letters 1914-1921*, p. 381). But he did profoundly understand prayer, and "the mystery of the kneeling, of the deeply-kneeling man—the fact that he is spiritually greater than the man who stands"; and it is primarily because of this understanding that he is to be called a religious poet. His whole life may be regarded, in one sense, as an effort to pray truly, and his whole art as an offering to God. At one time he compared himself to "a man gathering mushrooms and healing herbs among weeds; he looks bent and busied about something of little worth, while round about the tree trunks stand and adore. But the time will come when I prepare the drink; and that other time when I bring up the brew in which everything is condensed and combined, all that is most poisonous and deadly, for the sake of its strength; bring it up to God, that he may quench his thirst and feel his splendour flowing in his veins" (*Letters 1907-1914*, p. 48).

NOTE 18, PAGE 30

Kappus prints the sonnet in question at the end of the letter. It might be the poem of any sincere but not particularly gifted young man: it is neither very bad nor very good. The following English version, by Frances Cornford, gives a fair enough indication of its quality:

SONNET

Sorrow trembles down my spirit's ways—
Uncomplaining, dark as night she seems;
Snowy-pure, like blossom, are my dreams,
Consecration of my stillest days.

Often, though, the great unanswered Why
Bars my way, and I grow small and quake,
As before the waters of a lake
Whose deep waves I do not dare to try.

Then a grief descends on me more grey
Than a gleamless night of summer cloud,
Faintly lighted by one shimmering star.

My hands grope for love and lose their way;
There are sounds I long to pray aloud,
Yet my hot mouth knows not what they are.

NOTE 19, PAGE 31

The difficulty of love is a theme to which Rilke constantly recurs; it is impossible not to see in it some self-revelation,

perhaps a degree of self-accusation. Rilke had no Faustina to
teach him what Goethe had learnt in Rome; he could love in
a complicated way, but not simply or spontaneously. It is not
the inadequacy of mankind, but of man, for love that Rilke
laments. In *Malte Laurids Brigge* he says of women that "they
have for centuries undertaken the whole of love, they have
always played the whole dialogue, both parts. For man has only
repeated their lines, and badly. . . . But now that so much is
changing, is it not for us to change ourselves? Could we not try
to develop ourselves a little, and take upon ourselves slowly, bit
by bit, our share of work in love? . . . We are spoiled by easy
enjoyment like all dilettanti. . . ." He felt keenly the frustration
of "never being one with the beloved". The cry from one of his
letters: "How is it possible to live, when the very elements of
this life are completely incomprehensible to us? When con-
tinually we are inadequate in loving, uncertain in resolution, and
incapable of facing death, how is it possible to exist?" (*Letters
1914-1921*, p. 86) is surely one of the most despairing to come
from any poet since the terrible epigrams of Palladas. Rilke has
been held to be a fine interpreter of woman's love; it certainly
fascinated him, as his translations from Louïze Labé and Elizabeth
Browning shew. He had a profoundly sacramental view of
bodily delight, as one more means of that "transforming" which
he held to be the highest task of man. He could never rest content
with what he felt to be a mere succedaneum, the apprentice-work
of passion. Like D. H. Lawrence he hymned the body, and like
him he was always disappointed. It will be fitting to close this
note with something that he wrote a few months after he had
married Clara Westhoff. "I am of opinion that 'marriage' as
such does not deserve so much emphasis as has fallen to it through
the conventional development of its nature. It nevers enters any-
one's mind to demand of an individual that he be 'happy',—but
when a man marries, people are much astonished if he is not!
(And besides, it is really not at all important to be happy, either
as individual or as married man.) Marriage is in many points a
simplification of the circumstances of life, and the joining
together naturally adds up the strengths and wills of two young
people so that they seem when united to stretch further into the

future than before.—Only, those are sensations that cannot be lived on. Marriage is above all a new task and a new seriousness, —a new demand and question for the strength and goodness of both the people concerned and a great new danger for both.

"The aim of marriage, as I feel it, is not by means of demolition and overthrowing of all boundaries to create a hasty communion, the good marriage is rather one in which each appoints the other as guardian of his solitude and shews him this greatest trust that he has to confer. A togetherness of two human beings is an impossibility and, where it does seem to exist, a limitation, a mutual compromise which robs one side or both sides of their fullest freedom and development.

"But granted the consciousness that even between the closest people there persist infinite distances, a wonderful living side by side can arise for them, if they succeed in loving the expanse between them, which gives them the possibility of seeing one another in whole shape and before a great sky!" (*Letters 1899-1902*, pp. 107-8).

NOTE 20, PAGE 34

Rilke's chief contacts with the New Woman movement were through Ellen Key (1849-1926), the celebrated Swedish feminist, educationalist and reformer, widely known, with a mixture of affection and derision, as "Europe's Auntie". In his twenties Rilke had held the view—always a convenient one for a man who does not want to have to bother about women's rights—that women need not be concerned with art since children were their creative work. As Nietzsche's influence upon him waned, he became sympathetic and concerned about the development of woman as a social being, as this letter to Kappus shews. He was already in correspondence with Ellen Key, who gave fulsome lectures on a wide scale about the poet and his work, and was so enthusiastic a reader of the *Stories of God* that he dedicated the second issue of the book to her. She was a large-hearted (and rather soft-headed) woman, full of sentimentality and eager to "manage" and improve people. Her views and her social writings are today as old-fashioned as those of H. G. Wells; but though she may be laughed at by a generation which finds her modes of expression a little embarrassing, she should not be despised—that generation owes a good deal to her pioneering. Under her vertiginous influence Rilke became a supporter of much that she stood for, both in education and in social reform; but his enthusiasm never degenerated into the easy emotional chiliasm which is characteristic of our time, and after he met her in 1904 he grew steadily cooler, until he found this Elizabeth Hitchener of his, once his "dear, dear Ellen", if not a brown demon, at least extremely tiresome. Exhausted by her niaiseries, he once described her as "nothing but the tatters of an old-fashioned ideal . . . a universal aunt who has all her pockets filled for those who find pleasure in jujubes and cheap sweets, but cannot allay a single creature's hunger with her poverty-stricken, already somewhat outmoded dietary" (*Letters 1906-1907*, pp. 32-3).

NOTE 21, PAGE 35

After nearly seven months in Rome, Rilke came north at Ellen Key's suggestion and was the guest of different literary families in Sweden for an equal period. He was full of plans for work: he was anxious to write a monograph on Jacobsen, and had already begun to learn Danish so that he might be able to read Jacobsen and "much of Kierkegaard" in the original. While he was at Flådie he began to translate Kierkegaard's letters to Regina Olsen.

Evidently Kappus had sent a letter to him at Rome, which was forwarded by Clara, since a fortnight before he answered it he wrote to her: "Thanks for Kappus' letter. He is having a difficult time. And that is only the beginning. And he is right about it: we have expended too much energy in childhood, too much energy of adults,—that holds good perhaps for a whole generation. Or holds good again and again for individuals. How is one to answer that? That life has infinite possibilities of renewal. Yes, but this too: that expense of energy is really in a certain sense always access of energy; for fundamentally it is only a question of a wide circle: all energy that we give out, comes over us again experienced and transformed. So it is in prayer. And what is there, truly done, that might not be called prayer?" (*Letters 1902-1906*, p. 205).

NOTE 22, PAGE 41

Rilke was happy and creative in Sweden, and some of his finest poems, including *Orpheus, Eurydice, Hermes* and the *Birth of Venus*, were conceived there. But he could write later: "I went then to friends in Sweden, who offered me everything that the most open hospitality can give, but they still could not give me one thing, that limitless solitude, that regarding each day as a lifetime, that oneness with everything, in a word the spaciousness which one cannot see the end of, in the midst of which one stands surrounded by the uncountable" (*Letters 1902-1906*, p. 309). Rilke never learnt the lesson of Goethe's Wilhelm Meister: "Here is thy America, here or nowhere!"

NOTE 23, PAGE 42

This was either a set of three poems, *Invitation, The Last Supper* (which he wrote after a visit to Leonardo's tempera painting of the "Cenacolo" at Milan), and *The Confirmands* (inspired by the sight of white-veiled little girls in Paris in the spring of the previous year); or more probably *The Lay of the Love and Death of Cornet Christopher Rilke*. Both of these were published from Prague at this time.

NOTE 24, PAGE 42

The previous nine letters were all written within a space of a year and a half, and there had now been an interval of four years, during which Rilke had travelled extensively and written much. He had published both parts of his *New Poems*, written the first two of the *Requiems*, and almost finished *Malte Laurids Brigge*; and he was on the threshold of perhaps his most creative period, fortified by the financial security which he owed to his friend and publisher, Kippenberg. He was back in Paris, which was—if anything can so be called—his headquarters; it cannot be called his home—indeed, it must be remembered that Rilke was in a real sense homeless all his life. Besides his native tongue and French he knew some Czech, Italian, Russian, Spanish, Danish and Swedish, though not English. "Everything English is far off and alien to me; I do not know the language of that country, almost nothing of its art, none of its poets; and I picture London as something quite excruciating"—as well he might if he knew the descriptions of it in Heine and Dostoevsky (*Letter to A. Holitscher* August 1904). He did, indeed, pick up some English on a visit to Capri in 1907, and even translated the *Sonnets from the Portuguese* with the help of a prose crib. But the poet who did not know *Faust* did not know *Hamlet* either (even in German). He later told his French translator that he had "learnt in a few months enough English to read Keats and Browning. But disappointed by these poets, he experienced at the same time such a revulsion against England and the English language that he forgot almost as rapidly all that he had just assimilated. He had realized that England was outside the magic circle of his experience and the possibilities of his nature. His memory thereafter rejected all that it had gathered, as if it had never existed" (M. Betz: *Rilke Vivant*, p. 56). If England was no good, America was worse; even the Things that "came crowding in" from there were etiolated, out-at-elbows and fake.

NOTE 25, PAGE 44

But he did, after all, end up there: the *Dichter* became an *Unterhaltungsschriftsteller*. As he hints in his introduction, Kappus later worked his way into the world of writing, and became the author of cheap popular novels, many of which are published by the Berlin firm of Ullstein. *The Man with Two Souls, Martina and the Dancer, The Artist's Wife*, will serve as specimen titles.

RILKE IN ENGLISH

Of American translations from Rilke's poetry, the best are by C. F. MacIntyre—*Fifty Selected Poems* (University of California Press). Babette Deutsch has done *The Book of Hours* (New Directions). The very literal unrhymed versions by Mrs Herta Norton, a volume of translations from the earlier books of poetry, and the late and important *Sonnets to Orpheus* (both W. W. Norton) are of the nature of "cribs", accurate but often extremely uncouth.

The following short bibliography refers only to books published in England, and is in any case not exhaustive:

I. Works by Rilke

Poetry

Poems tr. J. B. Leishman (Hogarth Press).

Requiem and other poems tr. J. B. Leishman (Hogarth Press).

Sonnets to Orpheus tr. J. B. Leishman (Hogarth Press).

Later Poems tr. J. B. Leishman (Hogarth Press).

Duino Elegies tr. J. B. Leishman and Stephen Spender (Hogarth Press).

Leishman's English renderings of Rilke are always skilful, and the best of them entitle him to be ranked among the great modern translators of poetry, Maurice Baring, Edward Marsh, Jack Lindsay and Arthur Waley. At its weakest, his occasionally obscure and mannered style is at least more like Rilke than are other translators' bluffer renderings. He knows the poet's mind thoroughly, and his very full notes and commentaries are first rate. It should not be assumed that his are the only good translations done; owing to the curious workings of the copyright laws, those by other hands remain at present unpublished.

PROSE

Stories of God tr. Nora Purtscher-Wydenbruck and Hester Norton (Sidgwick and Jackson).

The Notebook of Malte Laurids Brigge tr. John Linton (Hogarth Press).

Letters to a Young Poet tr. K. W. Maurer (issued privately).

Selected Letters tr. R. F. C. Hull (Macmillan; in the press, to appear Spring 1946).

The *Stories of God* are of no great significance, but *Malte Laurids Brigge* is a work of genius. The publication of a comprehensive selection of the poet's letters in translation (only the first, one hopes, of many) will clearly be an event of the first importance for a proper understanding of Rilke in England.

II. CRITICISM OF RILKE

Rainer Maria Rilke by E. M. Butler (Cambridge University Press).

A full-length critical biography; accurate, if acidulous. Professor Butler's German scholarship is beyond question, but her readers might be forgiven for supposing that she heartily dislikes Rilke the man. The book contains some remarkably fine literary criticism, particularly of the *Sonnets to Orpheus*, and some passages which shew a lamentable lack of taste.

Rainer Maria Rilke: Aspects of his Mind and Poetry, four essays by G. Craig Houston, William Rose, C. M. Bowra and E. L. Stahl (Sidgwick and Jackson).

These essays, by acknowledged experts, are all extremely illuminating, but the book is intended for the reader with more than a little German, since there are frequent (and occasionally very difficult) German citations. Even so, it remains the best introduction to the poet in English, apart from Leishman's excellent but rather scattered explanatory passages. Dr. Bowra's valuable essay has since appeared, in an expanded form, in his *The Heritage of Symbolism* (Macmillan).

A CATALOG OF SELECTED
DOVER BOOKS
IN ALL FIELDS OF INTEREST

A CATALOG OF SELECTED DOVER
BOOKS IN ALL FIELDS OF INTEREST

CONCERNING THE SPIRITUAL IN ART, Wassily Kandinsky. Pioneering work by father of abstract art. Thoughts on color theory, nature of art. Analysis of earlier masters. 12 illustrations. 80pp. of text. 5⅜ x 8½.   23411-8

ANIMALS: 1,419 Copyright-Free Illustrations of Mammals, Birds, Fish, Insects, etc., Jim Harter (ed.). Clear wood engravings present, in extremely lifelike poses, over 1,000 species of animals. One of the most extensive pictorial sourcebooks of its kind. Captions. Index. 284pp. 9 x 12.   23766-4

CELTIC ART: The Methods of Construction, George Bain. Simple geometric techniques for making Celtic interlacements, spirals, Kells-type initials, animals, humans, etc. Over 500 illustrations. 160pp. 9 x 12. (Available in U.S. only.)   22923-8

AN ATLAS OF ANATOMY FOR ARTISTS, Fritz Schider. Most thorough reference work on art anatomy in the world. Hundreds of illustrations, including selections from works by Vesalius, Leonardo, Goya, Ingres, Michelangelo, others. 593 illustrations. 192pp. 7⅛ x 10¼.   20241-0

CELTIC HAND STROKE-BY-STROKE (Irish Half-Uncial from "The Book of Kells"): An Arthur Baker Calligraphy Manual, Arthur Baker. Complete guide to creating each letter of the alphabet in distinctive Celtic manner. Covers hand position, strokes, pens, inks, paper, more. Illustrated. 48pp. 8¼ x 11.   24336-2

EASY ORIGAMI, John Montroll. Charming collection of 32 projects (hat, cup, pelican, piano, swan, many more) specially designed for the novice origami hobbyist. Clearly illustrated easy-to-follow instructions insure that even beginning papercrafters will achieve successful results. 48pp. 8¼ x 11.   27298-2

THE COMPLETE BOOK OF BIRDHOUSE CONSTRUCTION FOR WOODWORKERS, Scott D. Campbell. Detailed instructions, illustrations, tables. Also data on bird habitat and instinct patterns. Bibliography. 3 tables. 63 illustrations in 15 figures. 48pp. 5¼ x 8½.   24407-5

BLOOMINGDALE'S ILLUSTRATED 1886 CATALOG: Fashions, Dry Goods and Housewares, Bloomingdale Brothers. Famed merchants' extremely rare catalog depicting about 1,700 products: clothing, housewares, firearms, dry goods, jewelry, more. Invaluable for dating, identifying vintage items. Also, copyright-free graphics for artists, designers. Co-published with Henry Ford Museum & Greenfield Village. 160pp. 8¼ x 11.   25780-0

HISTORIC COSTUME IN PICTURES, Braun & Schneider. Over 1,450 costumed figures in clearly detailed engravings–from dawn of civilization to end of 19th century. Captions. Many folk costumes. 256pp. 8⅜ x 11¾.   23150-X

CATALOG OF DOVER BOOKS

THE BEST TALES OF HOFFMANN, E. T. A. Hoffmann. 10 of Hoffmann's most important stories: "Nutcracker and the King of Mice," "The Golden Flowerpot," etc. 458pp. 5⅜ x 8½. 21793-0

FROM FETISH TO GOD IN ANCIENT EGYPT, E. A. Wallis Budge. Rich detailed survey of Egyptian conception of "God" and gods, magic, cult of animals, Osiris, more. Also, superb English translations of hymns and legends. 240 illustrations. 545pp. 5⅜ x 8½. 25803-3

FRENCH STORIES/CONTES FRANÇAIS: A Dual-Language Book, Wallace Fowlie. Ten stories by French masters, Voltaire to Camus: "Micromegas" by Voltaire; "The Atheist's Mass" by Balzac; "Minuet" by de Maupassant; "The Guest" by Camus, six more. Excellent English translations on facing pages. Also French-English vocabulary list, exercises, more. 352pp. 5⅜ x 8½. 26443-2

CHICAGO AT THE TURN OF THE CENTURY IN PHOTOGRAPHS: 122 Historic Views from the Collections of the Chicago Historical Society, Larry A. Viskochil. Rare large-format prints offer detailed views of City Hall, State Street, the Loop, Hull House, Union Station, many other landmarks, circa 1904-1913. Introduction. Captions. Maps. 144pp. 9⅜ x 12¼. 24656-6

OLD BROOKLYN IN EARLY PHOTOGRAPHS, 1865-1929, William Lee Younger. Luna Park, Gravesend race track, construction of Grand Army Plaza, moving of Hotel Brighton, etc. 157 previously unpublished photographs. 165pp. 8⅞ x 11¾. 23587-4

THE MYTHS OF THE NORTH AMERICAN INDIANS, Lewis Spence. Rich anthology of the myths and legends of the Algonquins, Iroquois, Pawnees and Sioux, prefaced by an extensive historical and ethnological commentary. 36 illustrations. 480pp. 5⅜ x 8½. 25967-6

AN ENCYCLOPEDIA OF BATTLES: Accounts of Over 1,560 Battles from 1479 B.C. to the Present, David Eggenberger. Essential details of every major battle in recorded history from the first battle of Megiddo in 1479 B.C. to Grenada in 1984. List of Battle Maps. New Appendix covering the years 1967-1984. Index. 99 illustrations. 544pp. 6½ x 9¼. 24913-1

SAILING ALONE AROUND THE WORLD, Captain Joshua Slocum. First man to sail around the world, alone, in small boat. One of great feats of seamanship told in delightful manner. 67 illustrations. 294pp. 5⅜ x 8½. 20326-3

ANARCHISM AND OTHER ESSAYS, Emma Goldman. Powerful, penetrating, prophetic essays on direct action, role of minorities, prison reform, puritan hypocrisy, violence, etc. 271pp. 5⅜ x 8½. 22484-8

MYTHS OF THE HINDUS AND BUDDHISTS, Ananda K. Coomaraswamy and Sister Nivedita. Great stories of the epics; deeds of Krishna, Shiva, taken from puranas, Vedas, folk tales; etc. 32 illustrations. 400pp. 5⅜ x 8½. 21759-0

THE TRAUMA OF BIRTH, Otto Rank. Rank's controversial thesis that anxiety neurosis is caused by profound psychological trauma which occurs at birth. 256pp. 5⅜ x 8½. 27974-X

A THEOLOGICO-POLITICAL TREATISE, Benedict Spinoza. Also contains unfinished Political Treatise. Great classic on religious liberty, theory of government on common consent. R. Elwes translation. Total of 421pp. 5⅜ x 8½. 20249-6

CATALOG OF DOVER BOOKS

ANATOMY: A Complete Guide for Artists, Joseph Sheppard. A master of figure drawing shows artists how to render human anatomy convincingly. Over 460 illustrations. 224pp. 8⅜ x 11¼. 27279-6

MEDIEVAL CALLIGRAPHY: Its History and Technique, Marc Drogin. Spirited history, comprehensive instruction manual covers 13 styles (ca. 4th century through 15th). Excellent photographs; directions for duplicating medieval techniques with modern tools. 224pp. 8⅜ x 11¼. 26142-5

DRIED FLOWERS: How to Prepare Them, Sarah Whitlock and Martha Rankin. Complete instructions on how to use silica gel, meal and borax, perlite aggregate, sand and borax, glycerine and water to create attractive permanent flower arrangements. 12 illustrations. 32pp. 5⅜ x 8½. 21802-3

EASY-TO-MAKE BIRD FEEDERS FOR WOODWORKERS, Scott D. Campbell. Detailed, simple-to-use guide for designing, constructing, caring for and using feeders. Text, illustrations for 12 classic and contemporary designs. 96pp. 5⅜ x 8½. 25847-5

SCOTTISH WONDER TALES FROM MYTH AND LEGEND, Donald A. Mackenzie. 16 lively tales tell of giants rumbling down mountainsides, of a magic wand that turns stone pillars into warriors, of gods and goddesses, evil hags, powerful forces and more. 240pp. 5⅜ x 8½. 29677-6

THE HISTORY OF UNDERCLOTHES, C. Willett Cunnington and Phyllis Cunnington. Fascinating, well-documented survey covering six centuries of English undergarments, enhanced with over 100 illustrations: 12th-century laced-up bodice, footed long drawers (1795), 19th-century bustles, 19th-century corsets for men, Victorian "bust improvers," much more. 272pp. 5⅜ x 8¼. 27124-2

ARTS AND CRAFTS FURNITURE: The Complete Brooks Catalog of 1912, Brooks Manufacturing Co. Photos and detailed descriptions of more than 150 now very collectible furniture designs from the Arts and Crafts movement depict davenports, settees, buffets, desks, tables, chairs, bedsteads, dressers and more, all built of solid, quarter-sawed oak. Invaluable for students and enthusiasts of antiques, Americana and the decorative arts. 80pp. 6½ x 9¼. 27471-3

WILBUR AND ORVILLE: A Biography of the Wright Brothers, Fred Howard. Definitive, crisply written study tells the full story of the brothers' lives and work. A vividly written biography, unparalleled in scope and color, that also captures the spirit of an extraordinary era. 560pp. 6⅛ x 9¼. 40297-5

THE ARTS OF THE SAILOR: Knotting, Splicing and Ropework, Hervey Garrett Smith. Indispensable shipboard reference covers tools, basic knots and useful hitches; handsewing and canvas work, more. Over 100 illustrations. Delightful reading for sea lovers. 256pp. 5⅜ x 8½. 26440-8

FRANK LLOYD WRIGHT'S FALLINGWATER: The House and Its History, Second, Revised Edition, Donald Hoffmann. A total revision—both in text and illustrations—of the standard document on Fallingwater, the boldest, most personal architectural statement of Wright's mature years, updated with valuable new material from the recently opened Frank Lloyd Wright Archives. "Fascinating"—*The New York Times*. 116 illustrations. 128pp. 9¼ x 10¾. 27430-6

CATALOG OF DOVER BOOKS

THE STORY OF THE TITANIC AS TOLD BY ITS SURVIVORS, Jack Winocour (ed.). What it was really like. Panic, despair, shocking inefficiency, and a little heroism. More thrilling than any fictional account. 26 illustrations. 320pp. 5⅜ x 8½.
20610-6

FAIRY AND FOLK TALES OF THE IRISH PEASANTRY, William Butler Yeats (ed.). Treasury of 64 tales from the twilight world of Celtic myth and legend: "The Soul Cages," "The Kildare Pooka," "King O'Toole and his Goose," many more. Introduction and Notes by W. B. Yeats. 352pp. 5⅜ x 8½. 26941-8

BUDDHIST MAHAYANA TEXTS, E. B. Cowell and others (eds.). Superb, accurate translations of basic documents in Mahayana Buddhism, highly important in history of religions. The Buddha-karita of Asvaghosha, Larger Sukhavativyuha, more. 448pp. 5⅜ x 8½. 25552-2

ONE TWO THREE . . . INFINITY: Facts and Speculations of Science, George Gamow. Great physicist's fascinating, readable overview of contemporary science: number theory, relativity, fourth dimension, entropy, genes, atomic structure, much more. 128 illustrations. Index. 352pp. 5⅜ x 8½. 25664-2

EXPERIMENTATION AND MEASUREMENT, W. J. Youden. Introductory manual explains laws of measurement in simple terms and offers tips for achieving accuracy and minimizing errors. Mathematics of measurement, use of instruments, experimenting with machines. 1994 edition. Foreword. Preface. Introduction. Epilogue. Selected Readings. Glossary. Index. Tables and figures. 128pp. 5⅜ x 8½. 40451-X

DALÍ ON MODERN ART: The Cuckolds of Antiquated Modern Art, Salvador Dalí. Influential painter skewers modern art and its practitioners. Outrageous evaluations of Picasso, Cézanne, Turner, more. 15 renderings of paintings discussed. 44 calligraphic decorations by Dalí. 96pp. 5⅜ x 8½. (Available in U.S. only.) 29220-7

ANTIQUE PLAYING CARDS: A Pictorial History, Henry René D'Allemagne. Over 900 elaborate, decorative images from rare playing cards (14th–20th centuries): Bacchus, death, dancing dogs, hunting scenes, royal coats of arms, players cheating, much more. 96pp. 9¼ x 12¼. 29265-7

MAKING FURNITURE MASTERPIECES: 30 Projects with Measured Drawings, Franklin H. Gottshall. Step-by-step instructions, illustrations for constructing handsome, useful pieces, among them a Sheraton desk, Chippendale chair, Spanish desk, Queen Anne table and a William and Mary dressing mirror. 224pp. 8⅛ x 11¼. 29338-6

THE FOSSIL BOOK: A Record of Prehistoric Life, Patricia V. Rich et al. Profusely illustrated definitive guide covers everything from single-celled organisms and dinosaurs to birds and mammals and the interplay between climate and man. Over 1,500 illustrations. 760pp. 7½ x 10⅛. 29371-8

Paperbound unless otherwise indicated. Available at your book dealer, online at **www.doverpublications.com**, or by writing to Dept. GI, Dover Publications, Inc., 31 East 2nd Street, Mineola, NY 11501. For current price information or for free catalogues (please indicate field of interest), write to Dover Publications or log on to **www.doverpublications.com** and see every Dover book in print. Dover publishes more than 500 books each year on science, elementary and advanced mathematics, biology, music, art, literary history, social sciences, and other areas.